# THE FINDHORN BOOK OF

# Connecting with Nature

*by*
John R. Stowe

© John R. Stowe 2003

First published by Findhorn Press 2003

ISBN 1 84409 011 6

All rights reserved.
The contents of this book may not be reproduced in any form,
except for short extracts for quotation or review,
without the written permission of the publisher.

British Library Cataloguing-in-Publication Data.
A catalogue record for this book is available from
the British Library.

Edited by Elaine Harrison
Cover and internal book design by Thierry Bogliolo
Cover background photograph by Digital Vision
Cover central photograph ©Thinkstock
Illustrations by John R. Stowe

Printed and bound by WS Bookwell, Finland

Published by
**Findhorn Press**
305a The Park, Findhorn
Forres IV36 3TE
Scotland, UK
tel 01309 690582
fax 01309 690036
e-mail: info@findhornpress.com

**findhornpress.com**

# TABLE OF CONTENTS

| | | |
|---|---|---|
| Introduction | | 4 |
| Chapter 1 | Earth | 8 |
| Chapter 2 | What is Nature? | 15 |
| Chapter 3 | Start where you are | 22 |
| | Tune In | 25 |
| Chapter 4 | Natural rhythms | 31 |
| Chapter 5 | Child mind | 37 |
| | What's in a name? | 40 |
| Chapter 6 | Trees | 43 |
| | Relationship | 46 |
| Chapter 7 | The green ones | 53 |
| | Choose your path | 56 |
| Chapter 8 | The animals | 60 |
| | Lessons | 64 |
| | Losses | 68 |
| Chapter 9 | Topographies | 69 |
| | Perspectives | 72 |
| Chapter 10 | From the ground up | 77 |
| | Cooperation | 81 |
| Chapter 11 | Gaia | 86 |
| Chapter 12 | Humanity and Nature | 96 |
| Chapter 13 | Nature consciousness | 104 |
| Chapter 14 | Connect for life | 113 |
| | Broaden your exploration | 116 |
| | Activities | 118 |
| | Take action | 121 |
| | Into the world… | 123 |
| Suggestions for Further Reading | | 125 |
| Acknowlegments | | 128 |

# INTRODUCTION

I grew up in the "Big Woods." It wasn't really big – just a couple of acres between our suburban Philadelphia neighborhood and the corn fields on the other side – yet from a young boy's viewpoint, it contained the whole world. After school, on weekends, or during vacations, I'd escape to the woods at every chance. I scrambled after frogs and crayfish in the shallow creek. In a swampy area to one side, I marveled at mysterious plants like stinky Skunk Cabbage and weird-looking Jack-in-the-Pulpit. At the end of winter, I gathered furry bouquets of Pussy Willow. In summer, I dug sticky gray clay from beneath an old stump and fashioned endless "ashtrays" which my mother dutifully baked on the shelf in her oven. When it was hot, my friends and I would swing from the branches of tall beech trees, or climb so high within them that – hearts pounding – we could glimpse the roofs of our houses and the town beyond. When it snowed, we slid down a hillside until the ground was as wet and muddy as our soggy clothing. When my pets died, the woods offered a place to lay the bodies of hamsters, guinea pigs, a couple of ducks, and a big white rabbit. For ten years of my life, the Big Woods provided sanctuary, adventure, and education. Somehow, during that time, it also taught me what it feels like to love the land.

# CONNECTING WITH NATURE

When I was old enough to pick a career, I chose biology. I loved what I studied – from the elegant structures of the human body to the fascinating creatures that inhabit the beaches and shallows of the Atlantic coast. For grad school, I moved to northern Florida to study the ecology of freshwater fish. There, I entered an exotic realm of crystal blue rivers that burst forth from huge limestone caverns, a place where alligators lurked beneath the roots of giant cypresses heavily bearded with Spanish Moss. My love affair with Nature that had started in the Big Woods strengthened and deepened. After graduating, I got a job teaching biology. On the surface, everything seemed to be going quite well. Underneath, though, something wasn't right.

In theory, biology and ecology were supposed to help me get closer to the living world. In practice, most of what they involved was killing and measuring, transforming the beauty and mystery of the living world into numbers and equations. Ecological thinking is one of the best developments of the twentieth century, yet for me it wasn't working. My relationship with Nature was feeling more and more abusive and I missed the magic that had drawn me to it in the first place. Finally, I left teaching to look for a different path. To my surprise, what I found was therapeutic massage.

Massage and holistic healing showed me a whole new way to see the world. Practitioners understand that health depends on a balance of many factors – not only physical, but also psychological, emotional, and spiritual. I learned that manual techniques for releasing tension are greatly enhanced when we address the energetic patterns that underlie them. In the two decades since massage school, I've worked on thousands of people and have been privileged to study many different systems of healing and personal alignment. Each has its place, but one tool in particular became the focus of my ongoing explorations – the use of flower essences.

Flower essences are subtle energetic remedies that encourage growth and alignment at all levels of our being. First developed by Dr. Edward Bach over 80 years ago, flower remedies offer a gentle, effective way for individuals to understand and resolve the emotional and spiritual patterns associated with physical symptoms. Since Dr. Bach's initial work, people have been investigating the healing of flowers from every part of the planet. From the first day I heard about them, I was hooked. In 1984, I began an exploration of flower essences I made here in the southeastern US. In terms of helping clients, the results have been highly successful. In terms of personal satisfaction, they've been even more valuable. The deep, meditative connection with plants and environment necessary to make flower essences gave me back the heart-centered connection with Nature that I'd been missing for so long.

I've come a long way since the Big Woods, yet the journey has brought me almost back to where I started. From science, I learned how important it is to understand the way that we humans interact with the living systems that support us. From natural healing, I've learned how vital it is to inhabit our bodies fully and to embrace all parts of ourselves without reservation. Learning to connect consciously with Nature is the logical next step. There's no way to separate ourselves from the rest of the living world – the health of our bodies, our society, and the Earth are one and the same. To live full, healthy lives, all of us need to support a strong and healthy planet.

In *The Findhorn Book of Connecting with Nature*, I've tried to combine basic principles of ecology with suggestions to help you experience your own *direct* connection with the living world. Both parts are vital. Just as reading about massage is no substitute for the actual experience, merely reading about Nature can't give you the satisfaction, intuitive understanding, and meaningful insights that come from developing your own relationship with it. Reading touches your mind. The living world engages your body, mind, heart, and spirit. My goal in this book is to help you experience – in your own way – some of the joy and inspiration that the natural world has shared with me over the years. I hope you enjoy it.

John R. Stowe, *Decatur, Georgia.*

## Chapter 1

# EARTH

From out in space, the planet looks soft, like a polished jewel. Silver-blue oceans reflect golden sunlight through veils of wispy cloud. At the poles, massive sheets of sparkling ice lumber towards the seas with their loads of frozen moisture. Around the equator, dense tropical forests cloak the land in a broad green belt. Atop the ultimate heights, silver white snow dusts the bare gray rock of the loftiest peaks. Far below, where the continents reach the waters, constant waves alternately devour and caress the edges of the land. And everywhere you look, from the coldest mountaintop to the deepest undersea trench, from the broadest plain to the infinitesimal spaces between grains of sand, the entire planet teems with life.

Welcome to Earth. You live in the midst of an incredibly dynamic and vital world. Wherever you look, living creatures abound, going about their lives in a dance of action and interaction, connecting within one huge, vital network. All around you, an amazing diversity of species creates the biological systems upon which all of life depends. From the smallest bacteria to the largest of the mammals, each part of the natural world is inseparably linked with each other part. Each one fulfills its own special role in supporting the health and well being of the whole. Together, all these living creatures weave a planet-sized organism that is wholly unique, unspeakably beautiful, and imbued with wisdom and intelligence all its own.

You have a place here, too, an important place that is entirely yours. Wherever you live, you're inseparably part of this living planet. You belong here. Look around. Do you see oak trees or redwoods? Do palms, grasslands, or the stunted shrubs of the tundra surround you? Do you waken to the call of a desert owl or the chirping of sparrows, the shush of wind-brushed pines or the urgencies of rush-hour traffic? Whatever place you call home, the life around you is rich and vibrant and you interact with it every moment of your life. With every breath, you take in oxygen produced by the plants. You breathe out carbon dioxide, which those same plants use in order to grow the leaves that shade you and the roots and fruits that feed you. Every sip of water you drink comes from the same great reservoir – stored in clouds and rivers and oceans – that supports every other living creature. The foods you eat, the materials used to build your house, the fibers in your clothing, the cells of your body, even the paper to print this book, all derive from the living world. Everything you are and everything you have, you share with every other living creature.

You're connected not only bodily, but also through your mind, heart, and spirit. You have the ability to commune with the life around you, to understand its secrets, to access insights and information that let you live with meaning and alignment. This is your birthright and an integral part of being human. Eons ago, humanity was born within the embrace of this living world. Together, we learned to walk with the animals as companions and grew to awareness by focusing our senses on the garden around us. We learned the rhythms of sun and moon, tides and seasons, and adapted our behaviors to match their demands. We're hard-wired to notice the subtlest signals around us, from the calls of fellow creatures to the changes in the wind that herald a storm. We have a built-in capacity to receive the touch of this world, to be inspired by its majesty, and awed by its power. Our hearts respond to the beauty it shows us and our minds receive the lessons it shares. For many, many generations, these ways of knowing enriched our lives, infused our awareness, and ensured our survival. They live on still, within our cells – within *your* cells.

Most of us forget. We get caught up in the frantic pace of modern living. We let our lives be ruled by ever-accelerating clocks and try to fit more and more into the short hours they give us. We forget who we are and get sucked into such a round of appointments, bills, agendas, and news that we don't seem to have a moment to spare for ourselves. We live in manufactured environments on artificial schedules and listen for reports to tell us what the weather's doing right outside our own doors. We buy into the belief that the world is hostile and that humans are born to conquer and control it; in so doing, many of us find that life offers more stress, more anxiety, and a lot less satisfaction. Many respond with feelings of depression, or a sense that we've been separated from some vital part of our own being. We yearn for ways to feed ourselves deep inside, to reconnect with the people and the life with which we share the planet.

It doesn't have to be this way. The living world hasn't gone away; it's still here, all around us, exactly where it's always been. You can connect with it right now, if you like. You can reclaim your natural roots and access the peace and strength of knowing where you live. The advantages of doing so are wonderful and real. The world of Nature is life affirming; it offers a healing, vitalizing alternative to the activities and distraction of the modern world. The small amount of time it takes to go outdoors, calm your mind, and tune in to what lives around you pays off with benefits a hundred times greater. You'll find that your life deepens with new insights and perspectives. You'll feel recharged and revitalized as you let go of stress and bring your awareness into the moment. Your communion with Nature will help you open to the fullness of your own being. The shift will be felt in every part of your life.

How do you start? It's very simple. Start right here, right where you are – you're already connected with the living world. You already feel the call to go deeper or you wouldn't even have picked up this book. Take a moment right now to look inside and notice where the call of Nature is strong within you.

## *Experience*    WHAT'S SPECIAL?

*The living world touches each one of us in ways that are different and unique — and some parts touch us particularly strongly, be they places, creatures, weather conditions, or plants. What touches you the most? Allow the following questions to remind you what really attracts you to the living world. Jot down your answers so you can return to them later.*

*Jill remembers a place in the mountains:* "When I hike, I always sit inside a certain grove of hemlocks down beside the stream. I listen to the water and feel really secure. Somehow, everything seems more alive there. I feel really relaxed when I leave."

*For Barry, it's the turtles he knew growing up:* "Box turtles, they were called. I'd find them in the woods and sit real still so I could watch them walk along and sometimes eat. They hissed if we picked them up and pulled all the way back inside their shells."

*Pat has a whole list of things she loves:* "Thunderstorms, irises, waves on the beach, cardinal feathers, deer, dandelion puffs..."

1. *List some of the places that feel really special to you. How do you feel when you're there? What do you think makes them feel so special?*

2. *Which plants, trees, animals, or other living creatures have made the strongest impression on you? Are there any you feel really passionate about? Why? What about them touches you the most?*

3. *What concerns you most about what you see going on in the living world? Which of the environmental challenges that you know about seems to be the most vital to deal with?*

4. *What parts of the natural world are you especially grateful for? Which do you love? What parts of the living world are closest to your heart? How do you feel when you think about them?*

5. *Is there anything else that calls you to connect more deeply with the world of Nature? Do you, perhaps, want to live with greater vitality, or make a difference in what you see going on in the world? Ask yourself and see if anything else comes to you.*

# bOW DO I BEGIN?

If you choose this path of reclaiming your connection with the living world, you stand at the beginning of an adventure that will take you far beyond the brief introduction presented in this book. Here, we'll start you on your way with a framework of ideas and experiences to help you shape the journey. The text will present concepts to help you approach the natural world on its own terms. As you proceed, you'll have many opportunities to encounter the living world directly. "Experience" sections like the one above will suggest ways for you to move beyond mind and engage body, heart, and spirit. Treat these sections as suggestions about how to undertake your own investigations. Some will speak to you more than others. As you strengthen your own rapport with the living world, feel free to follow your intuition wherever it leads. That's the whole point of the journey.

We'll start right where you are now, by reinforcing the ways you already connect with Nature. You'll practice quieting your mind, stepping beyond day-to-day concerns, and starting to interact with the life that surrounds you. You'll explore different ways of perceiving. As you proceed, your investigation of your more tangible, physical connections with Nature will lead you naturally to consider some of the ways you also connect emotionally and spiritually. Ultimately, what you discover will be unique and personal; the insights and inspiration you gain will depend on your own interests and desires. Sometimes, what you learn will make sense immediately. At other times, your experiences will come by way of feelings, symbols, memories, or bodily sensations that might not translate immediately into words. Throughout the process, trust yourself and your intuition. Read the text, try out the experiences, and let them help you create your own path to the heart of the living world.

What will you get from the process? Different people have different experiences.

Brad experiences a sense of support: *"I feel stronger now when I take the time to be in Nature, because I can feel that the whole Earth is beneath my feet."*

Ginny speaks about the sweetness: *"When I pay attention, it's like I have all these friends around me. The feeling is really beautiful. I'm surrounded by all this love everywhere I go."*

Bill finds clarity: *"Time outdoors always makes me feel more aligned. I have time to listen to the quiet voice inside me that knows the way to go."*

Patti likes the sense of ongoing adventure: *"I feel that I'm part of something bigger, something conscious and aware. I can feel it leading me forward. I don't always know where I'm going, but I'm learning to trust what comes when I listen."*

Not everything you'll discover on this path will be sweet or pleasant. Tuning in to the living world right now can take you into deep waters. There is great beauty, powerful inspiration, and strong, practical wisdom; but – as you well know – there's also imbalance, disease, and a great deal of stress within the systems that support us. In fact, just as much as we need to connect with the Earth, the planet needs our attention in return.

What we call "Nature" is in fact disappearing very rapidly. We live in a time of unprecedented *dis*-connection, when the mainstream of society seems to have forgotten that we depend on the integrity of the living systems around us for our own existence. We've been brainwashed to believe that we're somehow separate from the rest of life, that Nature is our enemy, our slave, or merely a pile of inert resources waiting for us to use them up. We've let short-term material goals blind us to the consequences of our collective actions – and these are severe. Every day we read about worsening ecological crises from pollution to global warming, overpopulation to rates of extinction greater than at any other time in history. Each day, we lose enormous tracts of forest, mountains of topsoil, and volumes of fresh water – the very elements that support not just humanity, but all of life.

We need to turn the tide and we need to do it quickly. It's hard, though, to maintain a sense of hope and possibility when others shape our view of Nature. Unfortunately, too many of us get our information second-hand through the media – and the picture we get is definitely skewed towards the

# CONNECTING WITH NATURE

negative. Disasters sell newspapers and raise the ratings of the evening news – and because the challenges we face right now are complicated and serious, it's very easy to become overwhelmed by fear and despair.

To cultivate a realistic connection with Nature, we need to embrace not only the challenges, but also our own potential to make positive changes. The part of the picture that usually *doesn't* make the news is the level of delight and support that comes from a direct, personal relationship with the living world. In truth, connecting this way provides *exactly* the kind of support you need to deal with the more difficult feelings. The relationship you develop will feed you at your core with the joy of knowing that you really *do* belong here. It's like coming in from a long, self-imposed exile and returning to the embrace of an extended family you've missed very deeply. Once you re-establish it, your connection with Nature will continue to evolve and mature for the rest of your life. The roots you sink into the living Earth will sustain you with direction and purpose every single day. Your journey starts here, with a single step. Why not take it right now?

## *Experience*     NATURE STORY

> *All of us have had moments when Nature has touched us deeply. Sometimes these moments are as incidental as driving down the highway and catching a glimpse of a hawk over a cornfield, or being cheered by the sight of a rainbow when you've been sad or depressed. Other times, they can be dramatic and life changing.*
>
> *Bill talks about being a teenager and spending his first solo night in the mountains:* "I was terrified the first night, so jumpy that I'd wake up with my heart pounding at the slightest sound. Somewhere toward morning, I gave up trying to sleep, crawled out of the tent, and figured I'd just watch the sunrise. The stars were brighter than I'd ever seen in my whole life – and just when it was starting to get light, a deer and her fawn walked across the hillside above me. I was so still they didn't even see me. Somehow, that moment took away most of my fear. I felt so at home!"

*What about you? What do you remember? Tell yourself the story of one or two of your own most positive moments in Nature. When did they take place? What happened? How did you feel? Why do you think this moment was important to you? Write down your stories so that you can remind yourself of them later.*

Chapter 2

# WHAT IS NATURE?

Exploring your relationship with Nature will at times feel strange and exciting. There may be moments when your senses show you a world that seems exotic, fascinating, and entirely new. At other times, the process will feel as familiar and habitual as getting up in the morning or hanging out with old friends. And why shouldn't it? You're already deeply enmeshed within the natural world; you have been since before you were born. Every day of your

# CONNECTING WITH NATURE    15

life you've looked at trees, plants, clouds and sunshine – you already know what they are and long ago figured out ways to relate to them. Our goal here is to help you revise these habitual ways of seeing and begin to view the world through new eyes; that way you'll start to build a relationship with the living world based on the principles of *intentional connection*.

At the beginning of a new relationship with another person, one of the very first things you'd ask is, "Who are you?" You would then set about finding out what the person is really like. Before we go any further, let's take a moment to do a similar thing with your relationship with Nature.

## *Experience* — WHAT IS NATURE?

*Even though we use the word all the time, let's get a little more specific about what "Nature" means to you. Answer the following questions briefly and don't be concerned about whether what you say is "right" or "wrong." Instead, use each point to help you clarify what you already think about Nature.*

1. *In a few words, write your own definition of the word "Nature." Do you have any kind of personal relationship with it?*

2. *What relationship do you think Nature has with humanity?*

3. *What parts of Nature do you like the most? Do you have favorite plants, animals, or places? Do these have anything in common with each other?*

4. *What do you* not *like about Nature? Are there aspects of it that you don't trust? Do any scare you? Which parts of Nature would you rather live without? Do these have anything in common with each other?*

Most of us define Nature in fairly similar ways. My dictionary calls it *"The material world surrounding humans and existing independently of human activities and civilization; the elements of the natural world, as mountains, trees, animals, rivers, etc."* That's probably a working definition most of us could agree on. In popular usage, Nature is everything that lives apart from humanity, everything between and around the civilization we've built.

Now that we agree, though, let's look a little more closely. First, notice how much our popular definition of Nature implies a fundamental separation between humanity and the rest of the world. It seems to suggest that we could draw some sort of line in the sand and say that everything on *our* side is human, everything on the other side is "Nature." But can we really do that? Exactly where do we draw the line? If you have a garden, is that part of Nature? Is the same garden part of Nature when you let it go for a few months and all those native plants start to pop up between the rows? How about a deserted beach? How does it change when someone builds a small shack at one end? And what if the shack becomes a high-rise hotel? Is the beach still part of Nature?

We come up against the same types of questions when we look at plants and animals. Are the cats and dogs we keep as pets part of Nature? Are free-range cattle? How about antelope or bison fenced into pastures so we can raise them for meat? Are the songbirds you love part of Nature when they eat at the feeder you hung outside the kitchen window? Does Nature include all those pigeons in the cities? Does it include whales? Elephants? Redwoods? Pandas? Grizzlies? Most of these organisms are increasingly dependent on human protection for their survival. Are they still part of Nature?

Take one more look, this time at your own body. You depend on a huge number of other species in order to stay healthy and alive. Beyond the plants and animals that directly support you by providing your food, consider all the other organisms that feed *them*. You depend on millions of tiny creatures to keep the soil able to support plants, and on millions more in your own digestive tract to help you process everything you've eaten. You need natural systems to provide clean water, plants to keep oxygen in the air, insects to pollinate the crops you eat, and organisms to recycle your body's wastes. The closer we look at ourselves and the rest of the living world, the harder it gets to draw the lines.

To many of the people that inhabit this planet, the question "What is Nature?" wouldn't even make sense. Most people who live closer to the Earth than we do couldn't conceive of humans as being separate from their living surroundings. In their view, the world is a huge network of interconnections, with humanity representing a single strand among many. Although we do have a unique place here, our strand is ultimately no more important than any other. Here's how some of them describe their relationship with Nature:

"The land is our provider, our healer, and our inspiration."

*[Robbie Niquanicappo – Cree Indian, Quebec]\**

"We think of ourselves as custodians of the land, and the land's not just soil and rock to us. It's the whole of creation – all the land, water, and air, and the life everywhere – people, too. All these things are related and linked together in the Dreamtime.

*[Pauline Gordon – Aboriginal, Bunjalung tribe, Australia] \**

"The great beautiful thing I learned from the Lakota people is 'mitakuye oyasin': all my relations. When they say that, the way it was explained to me, it's so beautiful. It's so immense because it includes everyone who was ever born, or even unborn, in the universe, all the two-legged, the four-legged, birds, animals, rocks, and everyone who's here today. The trees, plants, mountains, sun, moon, stars, and everyone who ever will be born!"

*[ Janet McCloud – Tulalip tribe, Washington state ]\**

The dominant view of the world these days is based on the assumption that humans are fundamentally different from – and superior to – the rest of the living world. Such a belief goes back a long way, as far as the very roots of Western civilization. It has given rise to a mindset of domination and conquest, in which human ingenuity is seen as the only way to subdue an essentially hostile planet. This world-view has enabled us to create an astonishing degree of technology and material development. We've put people on the moon, plumbed the depths of the sea, and even peered into the innermost recesses of our own cells. We've discovered cures for once-devastating diseases, circled the planet with a web of electronic communication, and even cloned living organisms from a single cell. Yet, for all our ingenuity, we've lost some-

---

\* from *Simply Living: The Spirit of the Indigenous People*. Shirley Ann Jones, ed., Novato, CA: New World Library, 1999.

thing important. We've lost our sense of belonging.

If we buy into the belief that the living world is out to get us, most of our time goes into trying to distance ourselves from it. We attempt to build a technological bubble that keeps us safely "inside" and all the rest of life "outside." Even though what we're trying to do is ecologically impossible, the mindset behind it creates a sort of siege mentality. Paradoxically, the very walls that are supposed to keep us secure instead become a prison, cutting us off from our roots and robbing us of any meaningful sense of who we are. Deep inside, we miss the connection we once knew. Beneath the veneer of civilization, beneath all the activities we create to keep ourselves distracted, we've become a species that is desperately lonely.

So what can you do? Can you make the step from separation to inclusion? *Should* you? That's one of the fundamental questions you'll answer as you proceed on this journey. For now, why don't we hold *both* definitions of Nature. We'll use the word to refer to the trees, mountains, animals, and everything else that surrounds us. At the same time, we can recognize that the separation we've been taught to see between ourselves and the natural world is more illusion than reality. That way, you can take things a step at a time. Rather than trying to change your beliefs all at once, you can let the living world *show* you what connection feels like. From there, you'll be able to decide for yourself.

If you open to the possibility, you may be surprised at how easy connecting with Nature really is. Separation is not your natural state. Keeping yourself apart takes a lot of work. Instead of being something radically new or different, opening to the living world could be as simple as just relaxing into what you already know deep inside. What's more, Nature will meet you halfway. When you're willing to let down the barriers, you'll notice that the living beings around you seem to respond to your intentions. As you awaken the memories carried within your cells, you'll find the rest of life willing to embrace you. Inspiration and help will come when you need them. You'll notice synchronicities that the old ways of seeing can't explain. Connecting with Nature is not a journey you take alone. Indeed, you'll meet guides and companions at every turn.

As you get started, ask yourself who might be *your* guide? Is it the hummingbird outside your window whose sparkling flight invites your eye to follow? Might it be the tree in your yard that stretches its limbs toward the sunshine and reminds you to do the same? Could it be a child who asks you to take her on an adventure in the park? Might it be your own heart that longs to dance in a world of wild beauty? Whoever calls, take time to listen. Dare to break out of the old ways and open yourself to a more natural way of being.

## *Experience*      NATURE JOURNAL

*Your journey of connection with the natural world is going to take you into new territory. It will lead you to discoveries, insights, beauty, and new ways of seeing yourself and your place in the world. One of the most effective ways to help yourself along the way is to record your experiences in a journal. Keeping a Nature journal is simple – all you need is a notebook or sketchpad and the willingness to spend a little time with it on a regular basis. It is also deceptively powerful. As you record your experiences, you stand in witness to your own progress. This process of honoring what is important to you will actually make your journey much more profound and meaningful.*

*What will you put in your Nature journal? There aren't any real rules. Put into it whatever grabs your attention. Record the discoveries you make as you proceed through the experiences in this book. Make notes. Write down your observations. Put in some sketches. Glue in some dried flowers, pressed leaves, or a patch of snakeskin that you found in the woods. Try capturing in watercolors the hue of the sky as the night gives way to sunrise.*

*Journaling gives you a way to savor the aspects of the living world that add texture and richness to your life. Record them as if you were sharing them with someone who'd never seen them. Note the colors, textures, sounds, feelings, and details that touch you most deeply. You don't need to be eloquent – this isn't for publication. Just record whatever's meaningful for you.*

*Examples:*

*"This morning the goldfish in the pond were really active. They splashed in the spray from the fountain and swam in circles around the irises. When they swam beside each other, they looked like they were practicing some kind of synchronized swimming. It made me smile. I watched for fifteen minutes."*

*"The blue jays were really warmed up today. They did that little cooing song, where they all warble and bubble as if they were making music together. When the cat came outside, one of them made a really loud squawk and they all flew off together."*

*"The first crocus bloomed this morning. There was snow around it, but it still came out purple and white. The parts in the middle are so orange, they look like they're shining."*

*"It thundered all night, big deep booms. The house shook. This morning, the air seems so fresh and clean. The sunlight is sparkling on all the drops on the leaves."*

*Why not start right now? Get a notebook or small sketchpad that you can use as your Nature journal. It doesn't need to be fancy, though it could be. Just find something that you can carry easily and write in whenever you want. Use your Nature journal to record the experiences that make up your journey of connection. Use it to record whatever else you discover in the living world that gives you satisfaction, insight, meaning, and joy.*

There's a magic that comes from this kind of recording. As you put your full attention on it, whatever you're witnessing comes more fully into your awareness. Later, you'll remember it in greater detail, even before you go back and reread your journal. The notes you make are like gifts to yourself. Enjoy the giving – and the receiving.

## Chapter 3

# START WHERE YOU ARE

One of the wonderful things about connecting with the living world is that it's right here, all around you, right now. You don't need to drive hundreds of miles or buy a plane ticket to some special place where Nature lives. You don't need a lot of expensive equipment or years of special training. You can start to connect more consciously with the natural world when and wherever you want. In fact, you're already a lot more connected than you think.

Many people imagine that to have a meaningful relationship with Nature, they have to travel great distances and get as far from modern civilization as possible. A thriving international business in Nature tourism takes many people each year to well-known destinations where they can "discover" the grandeur of the scenery, the wildness of the animals, or the "unspoiled" culture of the people who live there. Which of these places captures *your* imagination? Would you like to visit the snowy peaks of the Himalayas, cruise the Amazonian jungle, or discover the unique wildlife of an African savannah? Would you rather fish for trout in a misty Scottish river, watch seals and penguins in the Galapagos, or soak up the sun on a Caribbean beach? There's nothing wrong with going to these places. Indeed, you could visit any one of them and have a wonderful experience, perhaps even something significant and life altering. All the same, it's not necessary. You can have a meaningful relationship with Nature right at home.

Look around you. Where is the living world already part of your day-to-day reality? Is there a park in your neighborhood that you and your dog like to explore? Do you have a garden where you grow flowers or vegetables? Do you fill your home with plants, sunlight, and fresh air? Do you notice the chirping chorus with which the songbirds greet the dawn? Have you ever tried to decipher the discussion of a group of crows in the back yard? Is there a special place you go to "get away from it all" and recharge for a few days? Pay attention to these seemingly ordinary connections. All of them are good places to start deepening your exploration; all it takes is to learn to experience them from a different perspective.

Have you ever noticed how when you travel to a new place everything you experience seems just a bit more intense than usual? Whether you visit a different city, a dramatic natural setting, or somewhere else outside your everyday reality, the very foreignness of the environment does something to awaken your senses. Colors seem brighter, tastes stronger, aromas more fragrant – everything appears just a little bigger than life. Why? It's because whenever you step outside your normal routines, your body and mind no longer know exactly what to expect from the surroundings. In response, they step their awareness up a notch in order to gather as much information as possible. What if you could call forth the same degree of awareness at home? If you could, you'd be able to approach the natural world – and every other part of your life – with heightened sensitivity. You'd get more from life because you'd be more present for it.

Would you consider taking a trip once a week to visit the realm of Nature? What if you could make it something special and unexpected, something that would let you experience life from a new perspective? You can do it any time you like, just by giving yourself regular Nature time.

No matter how much you want to connect with Nature by reading about it, the only way to really do so is to go right to the source. At the very least, that means going outdoors to where you can focus on the living creatures that share your world. It means taking time out from your busy schedule and leaving behind the phone, the pager, and all the other voices of civilization that clamor for your attention. Most of the natural world lives according to rhythms that have very little to do with the artificial schedules governing human society. To connect more consciously, you'll need to shift gears, slow down, and cultivate a sense of calm receptivity.

Something happens when you step outside your normal routines. Though it might take a little time to do so, your mind will grow quieter. Your body will relax. You'll find that your priorities shift and that you begin to notice things you'd overlooked before – the brilliant green back of a caterpillar, the soft breeze on your skin, the slow movement of the sun across the sky. If you let yourself enjoy it, you'll find that Nature time leaves you deeply refreshed. You'll return to the rest of your life feeling revitalized and stronger.

Nature time is your chance to commune with what lives around you. It could be as simple as sitting in your back yard or walking in a nearby park. Sometimes, though, you'll want to go a little farther away. Find a natural area outside the city. Take a day at the beach or a weekend in the mountains. Spend time where human development is less dense and natural systems more in evidence. These times will feed you deeply.

How structured you make your Nature time is up to you. Sometimes, you'll use it for activities that involve planning and organization. You might take a hike, canoe down a river, or explore the experiences outlined in this book. You might go out with a group of friends to identify birds or camp in the woods beside a waterfall. Other times, you'll want your Nature time to be unstructured and non-directed. You might take time to sit beneath a tree and observe what's going on around you. You could give yourself permission to wander like a child, pausing to investigate whatever catches your attention. "What's under that leaf? Listen to the sound of the water! I could take a nap, right here under this tree!" You could explore the Tune In exercises we'll outline in the next section. However you choose to spend your Nature time, use it in ways that you enjoy.

## *Experience*   NATURE TIME

*Make a commitment to spend at least one hour per week outdoors for the duration of this journey. You could be there longer or more often if you like, but keep one hour per week as the minimum. Be creative about setting aside the time if you need to; write it into your appointment calendar and check it off each week when you've done it.*

*Nature time is a chance to get out of your normal routines. The time is yours to use, just as you like. Choose activities that bring you pleasure – some of the experiences outlined here or others that appeal to you. At the end of each session, jot any insights or observations into your Nature journal. Enjoy! Quality time in Nature is one of the best gifts you'll ever give yourself.*

# TUNE IN

Once you decide to experience Nature more directly, how do you start? A good first step is to slow down and focus on what's right here with you, right now. Most of us live as if we were running a race, huffing and puffing our way toward some imaginary finish line that keeps receding in front of us. The rest of the world flashes past at 80 miles an hour while we hardly have a moment to take our eyes off the road. No wonder we miss so much of what's going on! To connect with the rest of life, you have to jump off the treadmill and meet it where it lives.

Wherever you are, one of the easiest ways to slow down is to pay attention to your own body. Simply watching your breath will help you make the shift. Do it right now if you like. As you read, watch the rhythm of the inhale and exhale that accompanies every moment of your life. Feel how your chest rises and falls. Listen to the sound of your breathing inside your head. Even though you can control it to some extent, your breath really has a mind of its own. It represents one of your most direct connections with the living world.

# CONNECTING WITH NATURE

If you give it your full awareness, even for a short while, it will help you move your frame of reference from the hyperactivity of the mind into a more organic experience involving all your senses.

Following your breath lies at the core of the Tune In practice, which you can use any time you'd like to bring your awareness more deeply into the moment.

## *Experience*    TUNE IN

*Although you can do it anywhere, the Tune In experience will serve you better in terms of connecting with Nature if you try it outdoors, somewhere you can sit comfortably for 10-15 minutes without being disturbed. Initially, take as long as you like to get comfortable with the practice. Later, you'll be able to move through it relatively quickly as a prelude to other experiences.*

***a*. Slow down.** *Sitting comfortably, focus your attention on your breath. Observe it for a few minutes with as much awareness as possible, until your mind starts to slow down and you get a good feel for the rhythm of your respiration. Your mind may keep getting distracted and going off in one direction or another, but don't worry about that. It's just what minds do. If you notice your attention wandering, just bring it back to your breath. It's no big deal.*

*You might imagine your mind as a pond of clear water. As long as your thoughts keep rushing this way and that, they ruffle the surface of the water and you can't see anything that lies beneath it. As you watch the rhythm of your breathing, see if you can let the ripples caused by your thoughts get smaller and smaller. Focus your attention on the quiet stillness that lies beneath them. In time, you'll notice a sense of deep calm start to ease through your entire being. Just watch the breath, in and out.*

*Keep your focus soft. Of course you'll be aware of general sensations, but there's no need yet to focus on anything specific. Resist the mind's desire to analyze or understand what's going on. Don't worry about whether you're doing it right — you are. Give yourself permission to let whatever you notice flow easily through your awareness. Feel how pleasant it is to be in the world without the need to do or change anything.*

***b.* Vision.** *When you feel centered, move your attention to your eyes. What do they tell you about the area around you? Keeping your focus soft, do a gentle scan of the area. What are your impressions? Is it bright here? Shady? Dark? Notice the contrast in lighting from one spot to another. Notice the colors. Which catches your eye first? Which make up the general background against which the others appear? What's the general visual tone of this area for you? What else do your eyes notice?*

***c.* Hearing.** *When you've completed your visual scan, shift your focus to your hearing. Just as you did with your eyes, now use your ears to survey the landscape. What do you notice first? Can you hear your own breath? Is the general ambience of your surroundings noisy? Quiet? Comfortable? Can you hear the sounds of human activity? Traffic? Airplanes? Sirens? Which sounds come from other sources? Can you hear the chirps of crickets or the bark of a dog? Are the birds talking? Can you hear running water or a breeze in the leaves? Take your time and enjoy yourself.*

***d.* Smell.** *When you're ready, shift your attention back to your breath. What does it tell you about your surroundings? Is it heavy with moisture or dry and light? What smells does it bring? Are there flowers around you, or the aroma of someone's cooking? Does the air seem fresh? What else does your nose tell you about your surroundings?*

***e.* Touch.** *When you're ready, shift your attention to your body. What can it tell you about your immediate surroundings? Can you feel your posture? Can you feel where your body is supported? What's the temperature around you? Is there a breeze? Is the sun warming your skin? How does the air feel? Is that different from the ground beneath you? Gather as much information as you can from your immediate surroundings.*

***f.* Breath.** *Now that you've engaged your body and your major senses, take a moment to return your attention to your breathing. How is it now? Is it any different than when you started the process? If so, how? Is it deeper? More relaxed? What else?*

*As you complete the Tune In, notice how you feel in general. Notice your level of comfort with the process – it may vary from time to time, depending on what's going on in your life. What have you learned about yourself? What have you learned about your surroundings?*

Tuning in is a good way to calm your mind and bring to conscious awareness some of the information your senses are gathering at any given moment. In this introductory exploration, we focused on vision, hearing, smell, and touch – four of the "big five" sensory modes with which we're most familiar. Your body, though, gathers information all the time in many, many ways. In addition to the major senses, you have other types of awareness through which you and the world of Nature share information. Environmental educator Michael J. Cohen suggests a list of 53 separate senses by which you monitor qualities ranging from environmental conditions like time and motion to internal states like hunger, thirst, and stress. He even considers less tangible qualities like intuition, rationality, and spirituality. Whether or not you agree with the entire list, the point is that your body is operating on many levels at once.

Most of the time, we're only aware of a very small amount of all this information. Especially when we're in familiar surroundings, the mind tends to run on "auto-pilot." Unless you seek a particular piece of information directly – like "what's the temperature of the ground I'm sitting on?" – or something crops up that is far enough out of the ordinary to grab your attention, the vast majority of sensory input remains in the subconscious. This filtering process isn't wrong – it lets you put your attention on other concerns – but it does mean that a lot more is going on in your environment than you're usually aware of.

The Tune In process helps you wake up your senses and take a fresh look at your surroundings. If you practice it frequently, it will help you to approach the living world simply and directly. Consider making it a regular part of your Nature time. Think about using it at different times during the day, just to change gears and relax between activities; after work, or before you go to bed. Tuning in first thing in the morning – even if only for five minutes on your balcony or in front of an open window – is an especially powerful way to set a positive, relaxed tone for the day. Try it for a while. You'll like it.

## *Experience*    OPEN TO LIFE

*In order to focus more completely on the living creatures around you, try the following two techniques. For either one, go to a natural setting where you can sit quietly without being disturbed. Then, take a few minutes to center your mind with the basic Tune In process. Once you feel calm and aware, proceed with the variations described below.*

1. **Tune in to a plant or tree.** *Let your senses scan your environment for living organisms. What jumps out at you? It could be anything, but let's say you notice the maple tree across the way. Keep part of your attention on your breath as you focus on the tree. Approach it with a feeling of respect, because it is a living being just as you are. As if you were meeting it for the very first time, open your senses outward and begin to tune in to the tree.*

    *Use all your senses. What do you notice? Look at the colors. Notice how many shades of green there are, even within the same tree. Listen. Does the tree contribute to the sound landscape around you? Notice the smells around it. Can you detect anything? If you're close, use your hands to explore the different textures. How much information can you gather in this way?*

    *Then, use all your senses to observe how the tree connects with its environment. Where does it draw itself forth from the soil? Look at how the branches reach toward the sky. Notice the textures in the bark, the tiny movements of the leaves. Look at the overall posture of this living organism. Sit with it for as long as you like. Let it speak to you in its own way. Whatever impressions come to you are just what you're looking for.*

    *When you feel you've gained a strong sense of this tree, imagine thanking it for sharing with you, and then follow your breath back to normal awareness. Record any observations in your Nature journal.*

2. **Tune in to an animal.** *You can use the same process to deepen your awareness of the animals around you. Although they're usually more active than trees or plants, the basic procedure is very similar. Begin by scanning your environment until some animal attracts your attention. What is it? A butterfly? A squirrel? Let's say you see a blue jay. Allow yourself to approach this creature with respect, as if you were equals meeting for the very first*

*time. Then, keep part of your awareness on your breath as you use your senses to gather impressions of this living creature – color, sounds, smells, whatever. Let it speak to your body directly, rather than trying to understand everything with your mind.*

*When you feel you've noticed as much as you can about the jay's general appearance, let your eyes shift into "soft focus" and put your attention on its movements. Pretend you're watching a dance. See the movement of the jay's chest as it breathes, the quick alertness with which it does just what you're doing – engaging its senses to survey the world. See it turn its head, pause a beat, then maybe hop toward the ground. Watch the flutter of feathers as it lands, then the quick thrust of its head as it grabs an insect with its beak and eats it. Watch as it springs back onto a branch, brushes its beak on the bark to clean it, warbles a little, and then glides from the tree and out of your field of vision. Observing your own breath will give you a meter against which to measure the pace and rhythm of the jay's movements. It might not make a whole lot of sense to your active mind, but your body will understand in its own way.*

*When you feel you've gained a good feel for the "essence" of this blue jay, imagine thanking it for sharing itself with you, then bring your attention back to normal awareness. Record any observations in your Nature journal.*

## Chapter 4

# NATURAL RHYTHMS

If you were planning to visit a foreign country, you'd certainly learn what you could about the language and culture in order to make the most of your journey. In just the same way, as you set out to explore the realm of Nature, understanding some of the parameters you'll find there will help a lot. To communicate here, you won't need to memorize a lot of vocabulary or confusing rules of grammar. The language of Nature isn't built around words, but rather around direct experience. At times, comprehending the natural world seems a bit like approaching a fine painting; even though the artwork might affect you profoundly, the experience may not be easy to describe with words. Likewise, communing with Nature often depends on moving beyond mind and re-awakening senses you may have lost touch with. You began to do that with the Tune In experience. Now, let's look at your sense of natural timing.

Over the past few centuries, we urbanized humans have insulated ourselves more and more from direct contact with the natural phenomena that used to rule our daily activities. Especially since the advent of electricity, we've had the luxury of setting our own schedules by using artificial light to extend our daytimes far into the night. We've become so accustomed to having heat, light, and air conditioning available at the flip of a switch that most of us hardly even notice what's going on outside our windows. We do what we want, when we want, regardless of time of day or season. Not so in the natural world.

The vast majority of living beings operate according to rhythms and cycles that have very little to do with clocks. Have you ever seen a bird with a wristwatch? Even if they had wrists, neither birds nor any other wild animal would have any need of one. They know intuitively when it's time to sleep or wake, when it's time to eat, build a nest, or migrate. They know because they live enmeshed in a direct awareness of natural time.

You can live on natural time too, if you choose. Awareness of natural rhythms and cycles is built into your cells, just as it is for every other living being. In fact, our so-called 'liberation' from these cycles is mostly illusion. Amidst all the technology, our bodies still respond very strongly to them. If you don't believe it, look at the challenges workers face when they try to fill the nighttime 'graveyard shifts.' Look at how often we get sick when the seasons change or the way our moods are connected to day length and weather. Look at how our digestive functions vary according to time of day and just how closely our reproductive cycles align with lunar rhythms. Paying attention to natural time not only helps you relate to the living world more deeply, it also gives you a way to support your own vitality.

To start connecting with natural rhythms, look first to your own body. The most obvious rhythm here is that of your respiration. If you observe your breath move in and out, your attention almost automatically moves closer to home. Next, pay attention to your heartbeat, which pumps continually like the second hand on your own biological clock. If you turn your attention inward, you can often feel your pulse directly; if not, put a finger to the arteries in your wrist or neck. An even more subtle rhythm occurs in the fluid around your brain and spinal cord, which pulses regularly at six to ten times a minute. Other bodily cycles operate on a larger time scale. Look at sleep schedules. Everyone knows that most teenagers – and quite a few adults – would be happy never to open their eyes before noon. These late sleepers tend to view 'morning people' – who might be up and running five miles before sunrise – as members of some incomprehensible other species. In reality, their internal clocks are just set differently.

The rest of the natural world operates according to cycles entirely analogous to the ones in your body. Let's look at a few of the most obvious. To begin, consider the familiar alternation of day and night we experience as the Earth rotates around its axis. This cycle is the clock by which most of the planet's organisms arrange their schedules. Can you feel the rising of the energy at dawn? Animals do, as those that are nocturnal prepare to settle in for the day and others wake and become active. The same thing happens in reverse at dusk.

The cycles of the moon are a little subtler. Once every twenty-nine-and-a-quarter days, the silvery sphere swells from new to full and back again. Throughout human history, many peoples have watched the moon closely, timing their most important activities in accordance with specific parts of its cycle. When the moon is new or waxing, it is considered a good time for planting seeds or beginning new endeavors. The full moon signals the peak of the cycle, and the final waning sliver marks the time to clear away the old in preparation for a new beginning. Of course, there are many variations on the theme. At first glance, all this attention to the moon might appear to be no more than mere superstition, but consider that the moon's pull is strong enough to cause noticeable tides in all the world's waters – and even a smaller, but significant rise and fall in the solid ground itself. Consider how that pull might affect your own body, which is over 80% water. So maybe the idea that the moon affects us isn't so 'far out' after all. Just ask any elementary school teacher around the time that it's full!

On a larger scale, the revolution of the planet around the sun, coupled with the tilt of its axis, creates the rhythmic variations in climate we call seasons. Whether they bring changes in rainfall as in the tropics, or shifts in day length and temperature as in temperate zones, the seasons govern the life cycles of plants and animals alike. Trees and other plants have elaborate strategies for getting through the hard times – from setting seeds and storing energy in roots or tubers, to dropping their leaves and needles. Animals respond to the changes in climate and food supply with their own highly evolved mechanisms. Your own body may respond in similar ways, tending to put on weight in preparation for winter and shedding it again in spring. Whether grasshopper, ant, or human, each one of us has our own way of handling the changes.

As you set out to connect with Nature, don't just look at where you *are* – look also at *when*. What you observe about the living world can vary from moment to moment, day to day, and season to season. As you observe the organisms around you, try to discern how their activities fit into the larger cycles that surround them. The sense of context you gain will affect not only your relationship with Nature, but your ability to align within yourself as well.

## *Experience*     SLOW DOWN

*Find a quiet natural place where you can sit for fifteen to twenty minutes without being disturbed. Settle comfortably into this place and let yourself slow down. Imagine putting roots into the Earth. Let your focus be "soft" so that you feel unobtrusive – almost invisible – and let the quiet rhythm of your breathing slow you down, as if you were gently submerging into a flowing stream of natural awareness. Then, just observe.*

*Most of the time, our presence feels pretty hyperactive and disruptive to the other creatures around us; when we walk onto the scene, most of them stop their normal routines and wait to see what we're going to do. By sitting quietly for a long time, you are showing them that you're not a threat and giving them the opportunity to resume their activities. It may take some patience – fifteen to twenty minutes is just the beginning – but this sort of practice can let you be party to the private lives of many animals.*

*Jean loves this practice:* "When I first did it, I wondered if anything would happen. Then, after a few minutes, a robin hopped down into the grass to listen for worms. It cocked its head and found one. Behind it, a chipmunk poked its head from between two rocks and started filling its cheeks with seeds. It acted as if I wasn't there. It was really cool."

*You never know what you'll find when you get quiet. Sometimes it's as subtle as an inchworm on a strand of silk; other times it's more dramatic. Whatever you observe, the more you practice sitting in stillness, the more you'll gain a feel for the deeper patterns of life around you.*

## Experience   NATURAL TIME

*We live in a society that is addicted to time. The hours, minutes, and seconds marked off by our clocks have an almost tyrannical hold on our minds and activities. Of course, a certain amount of time-consciousness helps things to run smoothly. We make agreements to work together at certain times, to send our children to school during specific hours, and so forth. Even so, within the parameters set by these agreements, you can have some leeway – and in the process regain some of the connection with your own internal timing.*

*Try it out. During periods when you have the freedom to determine your own schedule – weekends, maybe, or in the evenings after work – take off your watch, turn the clock toward the wall, and let yourself flow on your own schedule. Instead of eating at 6.30pm sharp, eat when you're hungry. Instead of going to bed at the same time each night, sleep when you're tired – and wake up when you're ready. Exercise when your body wants it. Listen to your internal impulses and allow yourself to follow them.*

*Even when you're living on a tighter schedule, you can still play with your sense of time. Make a game of it. See if you can wake up five minutes before the alarm goes off in the morning. Stop wearing a watch when you don't need it. Ask yourself if you know what time it is before you check the clock, and try to figure how long you've been doing a certain activity before you look. The more ways you can find to exercise it, the more accurate your sense of internal timing will become.*

## Experience   CYCLES

*People who live close to the Earth generally know exactly where they are in the larger cycles of the planet. How aware are you of where you are in terms of natural time? Take a moment right now to pay attention to the natural cycles around you. Think about how they might affect your life.*

*1.* **Sun**. *What time does the sun rise? When does it set? Does the length of day change where you live, or is it the same all year long? If it changes, how does it change? If you really want a direct experience, get up each day at sunrise and figure out the answer without looking it up. If sunrise is too early for you, set aside some time to watch the sunset each evening for a few weeks. Many peoples say that these times are especially "charged" with energy. How do they make you feel? How do they change from day to day? What shifts in activity do you notice throughout the day? Choose one spot and visit it at various times of the day and night and see what you notice.*

*2.* **Moon**. *What about the moon? Where in its cycle are you right now? Of course, you could look this up in the newspaper or on a calendar — but why not see if you can figure it out for yourself by watching the sky and following the moon through an entire cycle. When does it rise? When does it set? How do these times shift as the moon moves through its cycle?*

*3.* **Tides**. *If you're near the ocean, you probably have a feel for the twice-daily rise and fall of the waters. Yet even if you live far inland, the water in your area — including that in your own body — 'feels' the tidal cycles as they move around the planet. Can you notice the tidal pull that's happening around you? If you can't (don't feel bad, because that would include most of us), see if you can figure it out by looking up the tides on both sides of you and extrapolating the times. Then, see if you notice anything subtler.*

*4.* **Seasons**. *Where are you right now in the round of the seasons? Is the life force in your area moving outward into full expression, or turning inward to rest up for more favorable conditions? How does that affect your activities?*

*Chapter 5*

# CHILD MIND

Your mind is an incredible tool. It has the ability to sort, categorize, and organize vast amounts of information quickly and easily. It keeps track of mountains of sensory input, both from the world outside and from within your own body. It manages abstract thoughts, calls up stories and memories, and helps you map strategies for navigating the intricacies of your life. What's more, it does all this with such ease that you probably take its enormous talents pretty much for granted. That wasn't always the case.

Try to remember back to when you were brand new in the world, back when you were still figuring out how things run around here. Just like any other child, you sucked up information like a thirsty little sponge. You'd ask questions like: "Why is the sky blue? Why are trees green? Why do worms crawl? What does dirt taste like? And why does it turn to mud when it's wet? Why do we eat lettuce and not oak leaves? What's this called? And this? What's that? Why? Why? Why?"

It's enough to drive any adult crazy. That's because we've already got it all worked out; our minds have learned to organize the complexities around us

# CONNECTING WITH NATURE 37

into a simplified map called 'how things are.' That's not necessarily bad, since it helps us respond quickly and efficiently to unexpected challenges. If you find yourself in the path of a speeding car – or a hungry lion – the last thing you need to do is philosophize about how the incident fits into the overall scheme of the universe. In order to survive, you need to run first and think later. The tradeoff, though, can be a loss of spontaneity and authenticity in other situations that aren't so life threatening. Instead of paying attention to the wondrous subtleties with which Nature speaks in the present moment, it's easier to see through a filter based on what we've learned from the past. Take a moment to remember how it used to be.

## *Experience*    CHILD

*Have you ever watched children explore the world? They're usually bursting with curiosity. "What's this bug? Why is this leaf on the sidewalk? What's underneath that rock? Look at that fish!" A walk with a child can be fascinating, a meandering journey from discovery to discovery with absolutely no sense of adult timing or direction. Can you remember what it was like when you were a child?*

*Jill smiles when she remembers her grandparents' farm:* "I used to go out behind the barn when I was five or so and hide in the tall grass. Nobody could see where I was, but I could still hear Grampa and my uncle inside, talking while they worked. I felt safe and protected, but wild, too. The grass was sort of like my friend because it kept me hidden."

*Think back to your earliest memories of the natural world. Did you have a special place outdoors where you liked to play? What kind of connection did you have with the other living creatures around you? Did you have pets? Maybe you helped in the garden? Were the woods behind your house a fantasy forest filled with elves and dragons? Did you like to splash in puddles when it rained? Was the vacant lot beside the apartment building a place where you climbed trees and captured insects?*

*Try the following two experiences as a way to recover some of the child in yourself.*

***1.*** **Remember**. *Write down some of your childhood memories of Nature. How did you perceive it? What were your favorite activities? Where did you love to go? What was most exciting about the living world? Brainstorm a little and see how much you can remember. If you like, write it as if you were the child telling the story.*

*Example:* "And the frog I caught was soooo big that it almost got out of the bucket. But I kept it for a whole day and caught flies for it to eat. The second day I put it back in the pond, because it needed to swim there. I could hear it croaking to me every night all summer."

***2.*** **Do a kid walk**. *Take a walk somewhere in a natural place and approach your walk from a child's viewpoint. Try to put aside what you already know about the world and see if you can immerse yourself in the immediate wonder of the experience. What's interesting here? Would you like to go off the path and climb those rocks on the hill? Would you like to sit with your feet in the stream? How about following that butterfly to see where it lives, or turning over a log to see what you can find beneath it? Maybe you'd like to build a small dam in the stream, then make a hole in it to let the water flow out again. Whatever your child wants to do, give him or her free rein for a while.*

*Pay attention to your feelings. How is it to approach the world this way? Does it bring anything up for you? What do you learn? What do you remember about yourself?*

Children are generally engaged 100 per cent with whatever has their attention. By the time we're adults, though, most of us have developed all sorts of habits that distance us from the immediacy of our experiences. We name things, tend to view them in terms of our past experiences, or tend to see them as totally separate from ourselves. Now that you've had a chance to remember what the world of Nature feels like to a child, let's explore a few ways to help you experience it now with that same degree of direct engagement.

## *Experience*     SEPARATION AND RELATIONSHIP

***a.*** **Separation**. *Sit quietly in a natural setting. When you feel centered, focus* *your awareness on one thing – a tree, plant, rock, or anything else that catches your attention. Using your senses, tune in to whatever you've chosen. For now, keep in your mind the idea that you and it are two separate entities. Notice how self-contained you are. Notice how what you're looking at has its very own identity. Notice how you're both there – two separate entities that happen to be in the same place.*

*How do you feel inside yourself? How comfortable are you? How do you feel towards whatever you're observing?*

***b.* Relationship**. *Now, change your perspective. Put your attention on the same thing, but this time notice how you and it are in relationship. Imagine asking permission to observe it. Notice how you feel when you ask and then 'listen' for a response. If you feel positive about it, tune in to this entity. This time, keep in your mind that you and what you're observing are in relationship. Be aware of the way you're associated with each other.*

*How do you feel now? How comfortable are you? How do you feel towards whatever you're observing? Are there differences from the separation experience you did first? What are they?*

*Record your observations in your Nature journal.*

# WHAT'S IN A NAME?

One of my favorite ways to explore the natural world is with a camera. When I first started, I'd spend hours and hours behind the lens. I loved to frame my pictures carefully, then play with exposure, depth of focus, and timing in order to capture just the images I wanted. I enjoyed the camera so much I got into the habit of carrying it everywhere I went. However, one day I had a realization that changed my approach. I was in a meadow in the mountains photographing wildflowers when I suddenly realized that I'd hardly glanced at a single one other than through the camera's viewfinder! I was so focused on getting good images of the flowers that I'd forgotten to watch how the color of the sky changed, to enjoy the fragrances, to feel the warmth of the breeze on my face. Right then, I saw how my desire to *capture* the beauty of the natural world was actually getting in the way of my enjoying it directly. Since then, I've tried to find a balance; I still take pictures, but I also give myself plenty of time with the camera safely in my pack. The experience feels a lot richer.

There are times when we allow words to get in the way – much like the camera. The mind likes to know what things are; it likes to know what to call them, and what it might expect when it meets them again. Naming things is very important to children. During the years when we're learning about the world most actively, our minds use the names to create a mental framework within which every thing has its own place. It's a pretty efficient system, like a giant card catalog in which everything is cross-referenced by name. The names help us to understand how things relate to each other and to communicate among ourselves what we've learned. Sometimes, though, our emphasis on naming things gets in the way of seeing them directly.

Once we have a general understanding of how the world works, it's easy to rest on our laurels. Instead of continually inquiring into how things are in this moment, we're tempted to reduce the awesome variability of the living world into a tidy shorthand full of simple associations. When we view the ocean, all the adjectives we've heard about it come to mind: 'deep,' 'mysterious,' 'uncharted.' Someone says "Nature" and we remember words like 'relaxation' or 'wild and savage.' Mountains are 'majestic,' humans 'intelligent,' and rabbits 'cute.' Maybe you'd come up with different adjectives, but the principle is the same. Each thing is neatly pigeonholed into the boxes we've already drawn. Driving through life, it's easy to glance at the terrain just long enough to identify the general outlines, and then color in the details with whatever we already know. Let's take a few minutes to try things a different way.

## *Experience*   SILENT WALK

*Go somewhere outdoors where you can walk for at least twenty minutes without being disturbed. You can do this walk alone or with another person. If you do choose to go with someone else, make the agreement not to talk once you've started the walk. When you're ready to begin, breathe deeply and allow yourself to open to the living environment around you. Focus your attention by watching your breath. Then, simply begin to walk slowly, consciously, and silently. When your mind wanders – which of course it will – just bring it back to the breath and keep going.*

*As you walk, let yourself attune to the world around you. Feel the Earth beneath your feet. Feel the breath as it passes through your nostrils. Tune in with all your senses. Avoid the temptation to analyze or explain what's going on around you, or to talk, sing, hum, or otherwise interact with the silence. Just walk and observe.*

*How do you feel after twenty minutes in this manner? Would you like to continue for a longer period? Try it again for half an hour, an hour, an afternoon, or a whole day. You'll be amazed at how differently you interact with the world without the constant need to comment or interact verbally. Try it and see.*

## *Experience*    NO NAMES

**a. No names.** *Go to a natural setting where you feel comfortable. Sit still or walk quietly and observe all the living organisms around you. Try to keep part of your attention focused on your breathing, because that will help you concentrate. Then, see if you can experience the scene without naming anything. Just observe. Feel. Smell. Touch. Notice what this place is like before you analyze it.*

*Your mind, out of habit, will probably rush to fill in every blank with a name – so give it a task instead. Repeat a question like, "What if this does not have a name?" Doing so will give your mind an important job and also free up different parts of your awareness. Stick with the task for five to ten minutes. Can you get used to viewing the world in this new way?*

*When you're finished, ask yourself how it was. Did it feel different from your normal approach to the world? Did you learn anything? If so – what?*

**b. Names.** *Staying in the same place, go back to naming things consciously and see how you now feel with this more familiar approach. Do you notice a difference between objects you know a name for and those you don't? Does your perception of the environment change in this mode? How?*

*Chapter 6*

# TREES

When an infant was born among the ancient Celts, the people planted a tree to ensure a strong connection between the divine and physical parts of the child's being. The ancient Greeks called upon the god Adonis, who was born in a tree, to give them the core strength of the trunk, the upward reaching soul of the branches, and the deep Earth connection of the roots. The Aztec and Maya peoples visualized the central axis of the universe as a tree that connects all levels of reality. Trees play a central role in traditional creation stories from around the globe including those of the Norse, !Kung, Iroquois, Christian, Sumerian, Germanic, and Korean peoples. Wherever they grow, trees are rooted strongly in our collective imagination – and it's no wonder. They are among the most distinctive and important components of the global landscape. They're also a good way to bring your exploration of Nature a step closer to home.

If you've ever taken a walk in woods or a forest, then you know how strongly trees can affect the environment. The moment you pass into their shade, the conditions around you change; the air feels cooler and moister – not only because of the shade, but also because trees pass enormous amounts of water through their leaves. When you breathe, the air feels fresher. Forests create such large volumes of oxygen that they're often called the 'lungs of the planet.' Because their roots hold the earth and their leaves both nurture and protect it, trees create deep layers of life-giving topsoil. They offer hundreds of different mini-habitats for other creatures – from the tiniest sunlit branches to the dark crevices around the roots, from the surface of leaves to the holes of nesting woodpeckers. Indeed, the more closely you look at a tree, the more apparent it becomes that you're not just observing a single organism, but rather a whole interconnected system.

Trees thrive in an amazing variety of conditions and habitats. In the tropical rain forests, vine-festooned giants reach so high they block the sun from the forest floor. In temperate regions, they respond to the challenges of winter by dropping their leaves and growing new ones the next year. In regions that are even colder, spruces and firs offer shelter to animals and birds through the harshest temperatures. Where forest fires are frequent, some of those firs have evolved seeds that germinate only after they've passed through the flames, a marvelous mechanism to ensure that new trees sprout only when conditions are most favorable for their survival. Junipers in the desert get by on the scantest rainfall, while mangroves extend the tropical seacoasts by pushing stilt-like roots into the shallow waters and excreting salty 'tears' in order to survive where no other plant can go. In the African savannah, elephantine baobobs store water like great-inflated tanks. In southern Chile, enormous alerces stand like sentinels of another time, just like their redwood cousins to the north. Bristlecone pines up to six thousand years old grace the White mountains of California like stark living sculptures. Wherever you live, wherever you travel, trees represent a most distinctive part of the landscape.

Where climate is suitable, trees are usually the 'dominant' organisms in an ecosystem. This means that they help to create and maintain the environment that supports a whole community of other species. In the southeastern United States, for example, deciduous hardwoods like oak, beech, and hickory tend to be the dominant vegetation. When mature, these trees produce conditions including shade, humidity, and rich acidic soil that favor the survival of their own seedlings over any others. Many plants and animals – from squirrels and deer, to worms and microbes in the soil – depend on these trees to maintain the conditions that allow them to thrive. Barring large-scale disturbance, the community of species that develops around these dominant trees is complex and richly diverse.

When dominant trees are damaged, say by fire or clearing, those left will usually help the ecosystem to recover over time. If the initial damage isn't severe, a forest will gradually reestablish itself via seeds from the surrounding area. However, if the disturbance is too great, the degradation can become serious and permanent. In the tropics, for example, traditional agriculturists use 'slash and burn' techniques to clear small garden plots. These plots are usually maintained for several years and then abandoned – such a practice allows for quick reseeding from the surrounding forest. If the cleared tracts are too big – such as those used for large-scale beef production – or maintained for too long a time, the outcome is much different. Already, large areas that were once covered with lush forest now support only very poor scrub. Others face the threat of turning to desert. Though the details vary from region to region, similar losses are seen in every part of the planet.

What about the trees in *your* area? If you observe them carefully, they'll teach you a great deal. Let's start by noticing the way that trees affect the general ambience of an area.

## *Experience*  TREES AND ENVIRONMENT

1. **Tune In.** *Go to an environment where trees make up a significant part of the landscape – woods, for example, or an older neighborhood or park where the trees are large and established. Find a place that feels welcoming and where you can sit quietly for a few minutes. Follow your breath until you feel calm and centered.*

   *Now, turn your attention to the trees around you. Pay attention to your initial impressions. Which trees seem to have the most presence here? Is there one particular type that seems to be more numerous or important than the others? Which of the trees around you attract your attention most strongly?*

*After your initial scan of the area, use the Tune In technique to take you deeper. Open your senses, one at a time. Watch, feel, listen to, and smell the environment around you. What sensations come to you? What stands out about this place? What's the air like here? The temperature? What do you hear? How would you describe the general ambience? How would you characterize the quality of this environment?*

*When you've gained a good impression of your surroundings, turn your focus inward. Follow your breath as you do a general scan of your own body. How do you feel here? How's your breathing? Are you relaxed? How comfortable are you in this environment? Do you think the trees and the rest of your surroundings affect you? Just notice.*

*Many people say they feel deeply peaceful, tranquil, or just more relaxed than usual when they do this exercise. One of my favorite statements came from a woman named Patty. Sitting in a grove of hemlocks in the north Georgia woods, she said:* "I felt as if I were listening to music, just beneath the level of my hearing. It seemed like the trees were playing the deepest notes, like the bass pipes on an organ. I couldn't really hear them, but I could feel them all through my body. I felt like I was melting."

*Whatever you experience is fine. Just be present with your own experience. When you feel complete with the process, imagine thanking the area, and then follow your breath back to normal awareness. Jot down any thoughts or impressions in your Nature journal.*

2. **Compare.** *Try repeating the same exercise in different environments. Choose from the following suggestions – or find places of your own – to give yourself the experience of tuning in to places where trees have varying degrees of influence:*

- *somewhere with large trees – different from the ones you explored in the first experience*

- *a field or parking lot with no trees*

- *a newly developed neighborhood where the trees are very young*

- *an urban street full of people, traffic, and concrete*

*In one or several of these locations, repeat the experience outlined in part 1. Once completed, compare your results from place to place. Could you sense any difference in the quality of the environment from one location to another? If so, how would you describe it? From your experience, what would you say are the major ways that trees influence their surroundings? What did you observe about your own experience in each of these places?*

# Relationship

We're now going to shift our focus from the forest to the trees themselves. Individual trees are a lot like individual people; each one has its own personality or 'energetic signature.' Each is a significant part of its community and makes its own contributions to the living network around it. And, as with any other part of Nature, each tree offers you the opportunity to develop a more intentional relationship with the living world. Let's look at how you can take advantage of that opportunity.

Nature responds to what you put out. Have you ever had the experience of walking into a room to meet someone and knowing, before they even say a word, just how they're feeling. "Uh, oh," you might groan inside, "the boss is in one of those moods," or "Oh good, the kids are in a better mood this afternoon." It's like a sort of 'sixth sense' that lets you know what's going on even before you pick up the clues provided by the person's posture or expression. The same thing happens when a dog or other animal senses that someone they meet is afraid or malicious. No matter how much the person tries to cover up their true feelings, the dog responds to the underlying energy. This same principle applies whenever you approach the living world.

Your experiences with Nature will be much more rewarding when you approach them with a sense of honor and respect. So how do you do that? At the beginning of any encounter, take a moment to remember that you are approaching another living being. Remind yourself that the two of you have an equal right to be here, and that each of you has your own place within the living Earth. Keep in mind that your goal is to create a positive relationship, and that any relationship involves participation from *both* parties. Your part of the relationship isn't just about *doing*, it's also about being receptive to what's going on for the other party.

Every teacher of Nature connection emphasizes the importance of attitude. Joseph Cornell says, *"If we want to develop an attitude of reverence for life, we need to begin with awareness, which in turn can lead to loving empathy."*

Edward Deunsing advises, *"It is important to remember that you are dealing with another living, feeling creature – one that may not be hungry, curious, or in the proper state to respond to your attempts to elicit a reaction."*

Michael Cohen offers one of the simplest, most effective techniques for reinforcing this attitude. Before you begin any encounter with part of the living world, he suggests that you *ask its permission and wait for a response*. You can do this aloud, or silently. You can do it with some sort of ritual gesture – as we'll discuss later – or just by taking a moment to focus your intention. Once you've made your request, wait a few moments. Notice what you sense in the environment around you. If the feeling you get is positive, continue your process. If you feel uneasy or unwelcome, move to another place that feels better. In the same way, you'll find that it's quite beneficial to complete any exchange with an expression of gratitude. A simple "thanks for your help," whether spoken or implied, will go a long way.

These are the same guidelines that work best when you want to communicate with other people. Applying them to exchanges with other types of living beings is just a small step. Does it feel silly to talk to a tree or a river? It doesn't need to. In fact, many people are quite comfortable in this mode. If you're reluctant, though, remind yourself that whether or not the tree or river actually 'hears' the words in the same way that you would, your actually saying them is a very effective way for you to focus your own attitude. When you're willing to do this, the quality of your experiences in Nature will improve considerably. Later, when you've gained some personal experience with this approach, you can form your own opinion about what's really going on.

## Experience    RELATE TO A TREE

***a.* Open**. *Find a comfortable natural setting where you can be with one or more trees. Sit quietly for a few moments and follow your breath until you feel calm and centered. Tune in to yourself and your surroundings briefly, until you feel aligned and aware.*

*When you're ready, look around you at the trees. Find one that draws your attention more than the others. When you do, focus your attention on that tree; move closer to it if you want. Then, ask the tree if it would be willing to help you. Ask aloud or silently, whichever feels more appropriate. Wait a few moments until you feel a positive response. When you do, proceed.*

*Note: If the feeling you get after you ask for permission is negative or uncomfortable, there is no need to analyze it or worry about why it came. Just respect your intuition and find another tree. Negative responses aren't common, but it is important to respect your feelings. When you find a tree you feel comfortable with, proceed.*

***b.* Engage**. *When you and a tree have chosen each other, open your senses to observe it. Notice the tree's 'posture' — how it stands in relation to the landscape and to the other trees around it. How does it make you feel? Imagine that the tree is expressing its own essence through a sort of slow-motion dance, so deliberate that your eye interprets it as a single gesture. See how it pushes forth from the Earth, how its roots support it. Feel the way that it pushes toward the sunshine, how it twists and dodges in response to its neighbors. Notice where it may have lost branches over the years and grown around the injuries. What can you tell about this tree by looking at it?*

*No organism ever lives all by itself. Who else lives on and around the tree you've chosen? Are there patches of lichen or moss growing on the bark? Do you see any fungus, either up on the trunk or in the soil below? Are other plants using this tree for support? Are there signs of insects beneath the bark, or the telltale holes made by woodpeckers feeding on them? Have spiders used this tree as a site for launching their webs? Are there nests in the branches? Look at the surface of the soil, too. What do you see there? Is there a ground cover of leaves or needles? What else can you notice about the tree? Gather as many impressions as you can.*

**c. Deepen**. *If you'd like to relate with this tree more imaginatively, try a few of the following exercises; each one will help you engage a different part of your awareness. These exercises aren't meant to be linear, but rather to engage your imagination. Whatever you discover will help you understand your own associations with the tree more fully.*

• *Sketch the tree in your Nature journal. Study its form and try to capture it on the paper. Don't worry about making your drawing 'good,' just let the process show you what the tree expresses through its shape and form.*

• *Dance it. With your body, adopt the same posture that you see in the tree. Feel your roots go into the Earth. Feel the support they give you. Move as the tree might move in the wind. Stand still as it might in the rain. Notice how you feel. What do you learn about yourself and the tree in this manner?*

• *Sing it. If this tree could make a tone or a sound, what might that be? Make that sound – if possible. How does it make you feel?*

• *Free association. Speaking aloud – and filling in the gap – repeat the phrase: "This tree makes me feel..." Say it over and over again. Complete it with whatever words come to your mind. Not all your responses will make 'logical' sense, but you'll gain a deeper feel for your own associations with the tree.*

• *Imagine that the tree is another human being. If you saw a person on the street with the same posture and personality as this tree, what might that person look like? How would they be dressed? What would their outlook be? What would you imagine that person's life to be like? Of course, it's all conjecture, so give yourself permission to play.*

• *Dialog. Imagine that you could talk with this tree. What would you ask it? What would you like to learn from it about itself or about the world of Nature? Ask and then imagine what the answers might be. Listen carefully. What insights would this tree share with you?*

**d. Complete**. *When you feel that you've spent as much time with the tree as you'd like, thank it for sharing with you. Bring your attention back to normal awareness and record your observations in your journal.*

*If you enjoyed this process, return to the tree at another time and repeat it. See whether your experiences change from one time to the next.*

Open to the trees and they will teach you. Start where you are. If the experience really appeals to you, you could get a field guide to learn their names. But even without such knowledge, you can still observe a great deal. Look around. How many different kinds of trees can you see? Looking at areas that seem undisturbed, can you guess which trees are naturally dominant in your area? Which are most important to the other species around them? What can they tell you about the environment where they live?

If you learn to look at them as individuals, trees will show you a lot about their world. Willows, for example, almost always live near water. Here in Georgia, we see redcedars growing in rows along the pasture fences, a sure sign that birds find their berries extremely tasty! Oaks and hickories grow where squirrels plant them, and squirrels live where oaks and hickories supply them with food. Coconuts grow where they've washed up on a beach, or where people have planted them. What can you learn from the trees in your area?

Whether you relate to them as beautiful scenery or as lifelong companions, the relationship you develop with trees will support and satisfy you every day. The following experiences suggest a few ways to take the relationship even deeper.

## *Experience*  IDENTIFICATION

*Buy a field guide to the trees in your area and begin learning what you can about then. Start with those that are biggest, most common, or most interesting to you. Begin close to home and then work outward so you learn about those that live farther away.*

*What does the book tell you about these trees? Which are native? Which have been imported from other parts of the globe? How do they change throughout the year? Watch them where you live to see if the book is correct. Which are the first to put forth leaves in springtime? Which push forth buds and pollen before the leaves? Which have flowers? Which produce nuts? Which are useful to humans?*

*Of course, learning about trees or any other aspect of the living world is a lifelong project. Proceed at your own pace and follow your own interests. Most importantly, enjoy yourself every step of the way.*

## *Experience*    ENERGETICS

*Many people enjoy tuning in to trees energetically, using terms such as 'grounded' or 'deeply centered' to describe how the experience makes them feel. You, too, can move beyond mental understanding and begin to experience trees with the rest of your being. Use the following suggestions as guidelines. Try one or both of the following, just to see what you experience. Don't worry about whether or not they make sense literally. Just be open to the sensations.*

1. **Recharge**. *Asking permission first, sit comfortably with your back against the trunk of a large tree. Pay attention to your breath and let your awareness come into your body. Focus on your back where it contacts the tree, on the base of your spine, and the top of your head. After a few moments, notice how you feel. Are you relaxed? Energized? Are there physical sensations? How do you feel?*

   *Gina loved this experience:* "I could feel myself wrapped in warm safety, like I was inside a big hug. I felt like I could just let go, melt into the trunk of the tree, and rest there as long as I wanted. I stayed there for just five minutes or so and then got up feeling really energized. It was like I'd had a long nap."

   *Many people use this type of "tree-sit" as a way to relax and recharge when they're tired or stressed. What does it do for you? Be sure to express your gratitude when you're finished.*

2. **Energy**. *Open to the energy of a tree through your hands. Find a place where you feel comfortable and can be undisturbed. Focus on your intention on the tree and be sure you feel welcome to proceed. Then, stand facing the tree, close enough to reach it easily. When you're ready, rub your hands together lightly until they feel warm, and then place them gently on the trunk of the tree. Keep your arms relaxed and pay attention to your breath. Try to keep your mind in 'neutral' – i.e. don't critique yourself or worry about how you look. Close your eyes if you like. Then, just notice what you sense with your hands.*

   *What you feel may be very subtle. Lots of folks report a feeling of energy – either as pulsing, warmth, coolness, or a 'flowing' sensation. Many feel very relaxed, once they get over worrying if they're doing it they way they're supposed to.*

*When he tried this for the first time, Bob was surprised:* "I could feel my hands pulsing. It was weird. They got really warm. I was pretty amazed, too, that when I moved them away from the trunk I could feel the energy get softer – and then strengthen again when I moved them back."

*Notice whatever you notice. Thank the tree when you're done and record your experiences in your Nature journal. If you enjoyed yourself, try the same procedure with different trees and see if you feel any differences.*

## *Experience*     PLANT A TREE

*If you really want to understand trees, take on the task of nurturing one yourself. In many traditions, planting trees is an act of service and an affirmation of faith in the future. Olives, date, oaks, and apples – none of these trees come to maturity for many years. The investment of time and energy it takes to plant and care for one is a gift that bears fruit for generations. Some people plant trees for the beauty they offer, others for the nuts and fruits they provide. Some plant them in honor of a child's birth or as a memorial to a loved one who has passed on. Others plant them to help restore environments that have been damaged. A particularly inspiring story is that of Richard St. Barbe Baker, a Canadian forester who in the mid-1900's organized thousands of people to plant trees all around the world. His work included a successful demonstration of how even the rapidly advancing Sahara Desert could be contained by the intelligent planting of trees.*

*Are you willing to make the commitment? Find a place where you can plant a tree – or several if you like. Look at the conditions and find out what will grow best there. Get a tree, plant it, and then take care of it. Water it. Love it. Nurture it through the cycles of the seasons until it grows strong and independent. This tree is part of your investment in the future. If you enjoyed planting it, why not plant another each year? Encourage other people to do the same. What a wonderful legacy to mark your own commitment to the living world!*

*Chapter 7*

# THE GREEN ONES

"You are what you eat," the nutritionists tell us, in an effort to remind us that a nutritious diet is an important foundation of good health. In terms of day-to-day choices, that means eating foods that support your own vitality. If we change our perspective just slightly, we could also say that if we, and every other living creature on this planet, 'are what we eat,' then we are all pure light.

Think about it. The energy you get from your food fuels every activity you ever engage in – whether it be building bones or brushing your teeth, constructing a house or dancing the tango. And the food? Either it comes from plants directly – as roots, shoots, leaves, seeds, and fruits – or from the bodies of animals that eat them to live. In fact, every organism on the planet depends directly or indirectly on the energy stored by plants. And where do *they* get it from? From the sun of course! The solar energy stored within the green realm forms the broad base of a living pyramid that includes not only the plants themselves, but also animals, humans, parasites, microbes, and decomposers. It even forms the nonrenewable backbone of our own petroleum-based global economy. So there you have it. The whole wonderfully intricate network of life on Earth is built upon the transformation of solar energy. We're *all* what we eat – sunshine.

Look at how many ways that sunshine gets transformed. Trees are part of the green realm, as are herbs, shrubs, grasses, vines, and algae. So too are innumerable single-celled organisms that float in the waters, drift in the atmosphere, encrust the bare rocks, and even live embedded in polar ice. The diversity and variety of forms within the vegetative realm is beyond description – yet safe within our 'civilized' world, most people are hardly aware of more than the few that touch us directly. We recognize *crops* like corn, wheat, rice, potatoes, tomatoes, and beans that we cultivate for food. Modern agriculture is built around a small fraction of the many edible plants species that could support us – and actually *do* support our closer-to-the-Earth brethren. We recognize the flowering *ornamentals* used to adorn our yards and parks, as well as the ubiquitous grasses we use for lawns. Again, these represent only the smallest percentage of the total plants available. Beyond that, apart from a few trees and 'wildflowers' we choose to approve of, most of the rest of the plant realm gets dumped into the disparaged category of '*weeds*.' Weeds are the plants we have no use for, the 'pests' we don't like. A great deal of our industry goes into trying to eliminate them. In the U.S. alone, we spend billions of dollars each year filling the environment with chemicals designed to 'control' or kill weeds.

Most people who live closer to the Earth have a much more refined and intimate relationship with the plants that surround them. Many of the indigenous peoples of tropical America, for example, grow garden plots that include high numbers of different species all mixed together – mimicking the way they'd grow in the surrounding forest. I remember listening to an anthropologist recently who talked about interviewing eight to twelve-year-old girls among the Maya in Central America. Some of these girls knew the names and general uses of nearly 1000 different plants. Can you imagine? Such knowledge may sound incredible to us – yet it's really just a matter of priorities. In a society that depends on plants for its health and well-being, learning the uses of herbs is a part of everyday life.

What if we could approach the plant realm with a similar attitude? That probably wouldn't mean stopping your trips to the store or the doctor; it would just mean putting more attention onto what lives right around you. Wherever you live, people once satisfied all their nutritional and medicinal needs from the same plants you see every day. Indeed, even among our most hated 'weeds' are many plants that can be quite useful. Consider the fact that dandelions are full of minerals and act as a gentle tonic for liver, kidneys, and joints; in much of the world, they're cultivated as a delicacy. Plantain, another scourge of the lawn, is a great dressing for minor cuts and stings. Clover is used traditionally to fight cancer; oat straw is a relaxant; corn silk is good for the kidneys; and burdock builds overall vitality. In fact, the majority of our modern pharmaceuticals trace their origins back to compounds found in plants. Even today, the World Health Organization estimates that nearly 80% of the planet's people depend on traditional plant-based medicine for their primary health care. Maybe the rest of us could learn something.

Don't be intimidated. The fact is there's a whole world of green plants out there – more than any single person could ever hope to learn. But you don't need to learn their uses – or even their names – in order to see the plants around you from a different perspective. All you need is a willingness to approach them with respect. Start small, right where you are. Just like the trees, the plants will teach you directly.

## *Experience*    DIVERSITY

*Even before you learn any names, you can gain a good feel for the number of different organisms that live around you. To start, find a welcoming natural place where you can sit and be undisturbed. Tune in to yourself and then open with respect to the living organisms around you.*

*When you feel centered and in alignment, focus your attention on a small area right in front of you. If vegetation is thick, your area might be a meter square – if sparse it could be slightly larger. Then, simply start counting how many different types of organisms you find in your plot. Look at all the different shapes of the leaves. Look at the various forms of the plants. How many grasses are there? How many other kinds of plants? What small animals can you see? Look closely. The more carefully you examine the area, the more kinds of organisms you'll find. Most people are pretty amazed at how much they can actually discover, once they get beyond the first glance.*

*The first time she did this experience, Eva said:* "It blew me away. I sat down and thought, 'Oh great, all I can see is grass.' But then I noticed a little spider crawling up one of the blades. And there were some tiny flowers over in one corner of my space and beside them I saw a caterpillar next to a third kind of plant. One thing led to another and by the time we were finished, I'd found more kinds of things than I'd ever imagined could be there."

*When you're finished, share your gratitude with your space, and then record your impressions in your Nature journal.*

# Choose Your Path

There are many ways to deepen your appreciation of the green realm. Each of us has activities that interest us more than others. How about you – what would *you* find most enjoyable?

• *Buy a guidebook and learn the names and natural history of some of the more common plants around you. Many people start with flowers – not only because they're beautiful and fragrant, but also because there are plenty of readily available books about them. Once you've learned about a few flowers, you'll probably also know something about the plants that go with them: where they grow, what they're related to, what they might be used for. It will give you a whole new understanding.*

• *Leaving names aside, you can start appreciating the plants in terms of their personalities. For example, there's a type of grass in my yard that's very common, yet not showy enough to make the books. Over the years, I've become quite fond of this grass – in part because of its soft pastel blades, but also because of the ease with which I can pull it up. When it's in the middle of the garden, that's what I do. When I see it somewhere else, though, I'm happy to leave it and appreciate it. I don't really need to know the name.*

- *Engage the plant realm through your other senses. Let the fragrance of the spicebush leaves or the juniper berries be your introduction to those plants. Learn to enjoy the deep purple color of the pokeweed berries that the mockingbirds eat with such relish. Appreciate the scarlet blossoms of the cardinal flowers, and enjoy the velvety softness of the wild mullein leaves or the crisp succulence of the jewelweed.*

- *Pay attention to those places that fall in-between the more 'civilized' parts of the landscape. Check out the gully along the road or the vacant lot beside an old motel. Take a walk along an abandoned railroad track or check out the stream that flows beneath the highway. These places, often ignored by humans, are exactly where Nature flourishes. Indeed they can serve as refuges for many species that can't survive in the more cultivated areas. If you pay attention, they'll reward you with a glimpse of their hidden riches.*

- *Observe the ways that the various plants fit into the communities around them. Which flowers bloom earliest in the spring? Which wait until late summer or fall? Which plants supply the animals with food or shelter? What are those seeds that the squirrels covet so much? Which plant makes the soft downy fuzz that the wren on your porch has used to line her nest?*

- *You could also start to read about the useful properties of the plants around you. How did the traditional people of your area use them? Is the wild indigo really good for dye? Can yucca fibers really be used for sewing, or their roots for soap? Is mimosa bark really a good sedative or echinacea root good for helping you fight a cold?*

Wherever you start, follow your own interests and make the exploration as enjoyable as you can. Becoming acquainted with the plants around you can be deeply satisfying. Step by step, your sense of place will grow stronger; your roots into the Earth will grow deeper and more supportive. Because you have a clearer frame of reference, you'll notice when you travel how the new landscape compares with the one you know at home. Eventually, when you walk through the world, you'll find that you're never really alone. Instead, you're surrounded by green companions that share with you the moments of their unfolding lives. Maybe one day, you'll smile at the wonder of it all – and that will be just the beginning.

## *Experience*  ADOPT A PLANT

*The best way to learn about the plants in your area is to start cultivating a deeper relationship with some of them. For this experience, start close to home, in a spot you visit all the time. Find something growing there that looks interesting to you. Why not those little white flowers beside the walk? What about the tall shrubs down at the bottom of the hill, or the vines climbing up the trees across the way?*

*Once you've chosen something, tune-in and ask it if it would like to teach you about itself. If you feel a positive response, start paying attention in more detail. Your goal is to develop a long-term relationship, so you can use the various techniques at your disposal over a period of time.*

*Take time to Tune In to the plant as you did with the trees. Open to it with all your senses. Tap your own awareness by drawing it, dancing it, or otherwise engaging your imagination.*

*Start looking at the plant within the context of its surroundings. Notice where it grows and what conditions it seems to like. Do you ever see it in the bright sun? Does it mostly grow near water or in the shade? How does it look over the course of the day? Does it stand taller when the sun is high? Do the leaves or flowers close at night? What sort of seeds does this plant produce? Does it grow alone or in a cluster?*

*Observe your plant over a period of time. How does it change from season to season? When is it first noticeable in the spring? Does it bloom? What do its flowers look like? Does it lose its leaves or die back in the winter? Does the same plant come back next year – or do new ones grow from seeds left by the generation before? What animals hang out around this plant? Does anything seem to eat it?*

*If it intrigues you, find out the name of the plant and do a little research.*

*Where else does it grow? What conditions does it like? Does it have any traditional uses? Is it related to any other plants in your area? You can be as thorough or as casual about this exploration as you like – the point is that you enjoy yourself. Whatever you discover, it'll give you a way 'in' to the world of the plants.*

*If you enjoy this process, repeat it with other plants. In time, you'll develop the habit of relating to the plants around you as the individuals they are.*

## *Experience* — NATIVE LANDSCAPING

*This is a long-term experience that will not only give you a deeper appreciation of your local flora, but also help you to make a positive contribution to the health of the environment.*

*Do you have a yard? If so, consider exploring the uses of native plants for landscaping. Native plants are those that occur naturally in the area where you live. Because they're already adapted to the local conditions, you'll find that most of the time they thrive with very little attention. If you can find ways to incorporate them into your own landscaping, you'll not only create an interesting environment, but also spend a lot less time and money on watering, fertilizing, and pampering plants that don't occur there naturally.*

*Start small. Do a little research. Which local plants might make good ground covers? Which ones have showy flowers or brightly colored leaves? Which provide food or good habitat for birds and other wildlife? With a little persistence, it's usually pretty easy to find this information from libraries, local nurseries, or extension services.*

*When you've learned a little about the plants, try one or two of them in your yard. How do they do? Do you like having them there? If so, gradually expand your experiment. Bring in other native plants. Find out for yourself if they are indeed easier to maintain than other kinds. Let your native collection expand organically, a few plants a time. In time, you'll transform your environment. It's an ongoing exploration, and a very enjoyable one.*

*George went for another approach – an interesting variation on the process of planting native plants – he decided to devote his yard to local plants with culinary or medicinal uses:* "At first, I didn't know much about what I was doing. I planted a couple of wild grapevines and some dandelions and lamb's-quarters for greens. My neighbor couldn't believe I was planting dandelions, since he spends about half his time pulling them out of his grass!

"The second year, I came across a book on Native American herbology. That really got me started. They used a ton of different local plants. I started looking around and was able to bring a good number into my yard. I don't use them all myself yet, but I've learned a few and have a great time showing my friends how people could live on what God gave them. I even had my grandson's class come by when they were doing a unit on Native Americans. I enjoy it a lot."

## Chapter 8

# THE ANIMALS

What comes to your mind when you think about the animal realm? Is it the dog or cat that keeps you company? Might it be the cattle and chickens we use for food? Do you see the big 'stars' – the whales, dolphins, pandas, and chimpanzees that have come to symbolize the endangered natural world? Do

Tel 01309 690582 / Freephone 0800 389 9395
Fax 01309 690036
e-mail info@findhornpress.com
http://findhornpress.com

# FINDHORN Press

Thank you for choosing this book. We appreciate your interest and support.

If you would like to receive our full catalogue of books and other inspirational material, please fill in this card and mail it to us.

☐ Please send book and music catalogue (you can also consult our list on the web at findhornpress.com)

☐ Please send information about the Findhorn Foundation in Scotland (alternatively, see their website at findhorn.org)

Please write your name and address here *(please PRINT)*

What is your email address? _____

to:

# FINDHORN PRESS

305a The Park
Findhorn
Forres IV36 3TE
Scotland, Great Britain

*affix stamp here*

you see cartoon characters like Bambi and Thumper or maybe the grizzlies and rhinos that some folks still dream of turning into trophies? Perhaps you look out the window to see the squirrels and birds that are your nearest neighbors, or watch TV for fearful images of man-eating crocs, poisonous snakes, or disease-bearing mosquitoes just waiting for a chance to attack unsuspecting humans.

Animals are probably the part of the natural world to which most of us relate most readily. Because they represent such a vast and varied group, and because our lives have been interconnected with theirs for so long, it's no wonder that our feelings toward them take many forms. Since the age before history when our ancestors hunted – probably to extinction – the mammoths, ground sloths, and other great mammals, we've depended on animals for food, skins, and more. We learned to fear the larger carnivores that returned the favor by feeding on us. Over the centuries, we've used animals to meet our needs for labor, transportation, companionship, and entertainment. Some we've taken as they came, others we've bred extensively until their bodies hardly resemble their original form. Now, we're tinkering with their very genes so that pigs produce human proteins and goats secrete the silk of spiders in their milk. We live in a world where humans simultaneously honor, fear, exploit, control, sentimentalize, demonize, exterminate, conserve, and pamper the other species with whom we share the planet. And, as with plants, our view of animals is framed almost exclusively by the lens of our own needs and desires.

For the most part, we've been taught to view the natural world as a sort of hierarchy, with humans at the top, ruling and dominating everything else. We rank other species as 'higher' or 'lower' depending on how similar they are to us. We deem those we find useful to be 'beneficial' or 'good' and label those that prey on or compete with us 'malicious' or 'bad.' Some few that keep out of the way manage to remain in neutral territory. Granted, perception depends on the viewer. For us to see animals without a human bias is probably impossible. Just for a moment, though, let's try to look at them on their own terms.

Animals are our sibling species, each with its own vital and distinctive place within the tapestry of life. Can we put aside the concept of hierarchy for a moment and see ourselves as part of a network? Can we imagine the living world as a web of related species, all of which – humans included – are equally important within the whole? From our 'civilized' perspective, that might be a tall order, yet it is an integral part of learning how to approach the world with honor and respect.

Ecologists use the term "niche" to describe the unique place or role of any species within its community. Niche takes into account the various ways that organisms share resources like water, habitat, and energy, as well as what they eat, what eats them, and the multitude of ways they interact with each other. Each species makes its own contributions to the functioning of the whole. Each one affects and is affected by those around it in a huge, ever-changing dance of movement and relationship. Could you look at the world this way?

## Experience    NICHE

*Choose an animal that lives near you and see how well you can describe its place in the community. Any species you choose will lead you to a deeper appreciation – so pick one that is easy for you to observe frequently. Choose a spider or a pigeon, a beaver or a stallion, a squirrel or the leader of a pack of wolves – though if you live where you can watch wild wolves, you might not really need this book!*

*Remember that each animal is an individual in its own right. If you've lived around pets or farm animals, you know that each one has its own temperament and idiosyncrasies. So does every other animal on the planet. Even though we might not be so used to observing the individual personalities of mice or mockingbirds, they exist just the same. It's just a matter of learning how to look.*

*From your observations, outline in your Nature journal the characteristics of this animal's place in the world. Does it live in a tree, a burrow, the air, or a pond? Does it eat seeds, leaves, worms, grass, insects, or other animals? Is it active by day or night? Is it around all year or just during one season? How does it interact with the organisms around it? How does it affect the environment? Does it disperse seeds, spread parasites, or pollinate flowers? Does it keep the population of some other animal in balance? Is it an important source of food for another species?*

*What other animals interact most closely with this one? How does their role differ from that of the animal you've chosen? Squirrels and chipmunks, for example, often live in the same area and both feed on seeds and nuts. Squirrels, though, generally live high above the ground and concentrate their diet on the larger nuts they find there. Chipmunks live in burrows and pick up the smaller seeds close to the ground.*

*How does the animal you've chosen interact with humans? Is it affected by our activities? What else can you determine about the niche of the animal you've chosen?*

*Of course, getting to know any animal well is a long-term process. You'll probably be able to create a general outline of this animal's niche in one or two sittings. That's enough if you want to stop there. If you enjoy the process, though, keep on observing. The more you watch, the more you'll learn. The more you learn, the stronger your relationship with this animal will become.*

## *Experience* — PERSPECTIVES

**a. Unpopularity**. *Make a list of your least favorite animals. Pick at least five. What are they? Mosquitoes? Snakes? Grizzlies? Spiders? Tell the truth — you're the only person who needs to know this. It should be easy to come up with a whole list.*

**b. New view**. *Choose one animal from your list. Keeping in mind that everything has a place within the network of life, do a little brainstorming. What could possibly be beneficial about this creature? What benefits could snakes, for example, be sharing with the rest of the world? What about spiders?*

*Gabby chose cockroaches: "I hate them, you know. I couldn't really think of anything good about them at first. Then I remembered my grandmother saying 'if you keep a clean kitchen, you won't have roaches.' I guess roaches help to clean up the crumbs and bits of food left over, like scavengers. And something must eat them, so they're contributing to the other animals. I could probably get around to admiring their* persistence, too – all these people trying to kill them and there are more than ever! Beyond that, I'm still thinking ..."

***c*. Observe.** *If you can, try to observe one of the animals you're uncomfortable with. Find something accessible – you don't have to dig your way into a rattlesnake den or stalk a wild grizzly to get the point. You could watch a spider in your back yard, a fly on the windowsill, or the cockroaches that have a way of coming up into your kitchen from the (dirty!) apartment below.*

*Once you find the animal, call a truce for a while and just watch it. Look at how it goes about its life. Remember that it shares the same basic concerns that you and every other living creature have to deal with – finding food and a safe place to live, finding a mate, reproducing, and staying alive. Look at the unique ways in which this creature has evolved to meet those needs. How well do they work? How might the world look from this animal's perspective? How do you think it would look at you? Can you learn anything from it?*

## Lessons

When you pay closer attention to the animals that live around you, they'll begin to teach you in ways that might surprise you. For eons, people in close contact with Nature have been learning about the natural world by watching the animals. Some of the lessons are quite practical. Maybe someone first decided to taste those red berries growing along the riverbank by watching how the foxes gorge on them every summer. Some early healer might have observed that wild goats always seem to know which plants to eat when they're sick and started to wonder exactly what those same plants might do for people. We're all learning together here – animals and humans alike.

Some of the lessons touch a deeper level. If you're willing to learn, the animals can show you qualities to enrich every part of your life. If you're raising children, for example, you might watch the otters and reflect on the delightful and necessary benefits of play. You might remember the value of industry and cooperation by watching the bees and ants. The cat might remind you to take time alone, or to lighten up and get the rest you need. Hearing a flock of wild geese passing overhead might bring to your mind the need for council and ongoing dialog with the people around you. Of course, this type of learning is fairly subjective. Depending on your background, perspective, and the animals themselves, the insights you gain from a particular animal might differ from what someone else learns. That's the nature of creative dialog. If you keep your intentions clear, your interactions with the animals around you will bring a great deal of understanding.

## *Experience*     FOOD WEB

> At the beginning of your next meal, take a moment to be quiet and reflect on the organisms that went into making your meal possible. Think about the plants, the people who grew them, the organisms that pollinated them, and the microorganisms that helped make the soil productive. Think about the steer whose body went into that burger, the cow who made milk for the cheese, or the chickens who laid the eggs for your omelet. Think about what they ate in order to be able to do so. Think about the sunshine that started the whole process.
>
> You don't have to take too long here. Just notice the web of connections that feeds you. The more you reflect on it, the more you'll realize that each meal is truly a big slice of life!
>
> Now, before your food gets too cold, take just a quick moment to feel your gratitude for it.

## *Experience*     INNER DIALOG

> *a.* **Engage**. *This experience is another way your imagination can help to engage different parts of your awareness. To start, think about all the animals you know — whether they live nearby or farther away. Which ones catch your imagination most strongly? Bats? Whales? Chipmunks? Skunks? The garter snake who lives in your garden? The wolves that howl in the*

*far North? Make a list of a few of your favorites, then pick one to work with right now.*

***b*. Brainstorm**. *Ask yourself what attracts you most about this animal? Is it the freedom of the wild goose? The power of the bear? The beauty of the cardinal? Try to recall everything you know about it, and then make a list of the major points.*

*Jim was called to bears:* "Bears are strong and solitary and very big. They know about the Earth because they always know where to find edible roots. They know when it's time to be active and when to hibernate..."

*Ask yourself honestly, "Why does this animal seem so important to me? What can I learn from it? What does this attraction show me about myself?"*

*This is an experience of imagination. For now, you're concerned with what this animal means to you, not what anyone else says about it. Avoid the temptation to be too literal, or to criticize yourself for what comes to your mind. Just observe whatever's there. Without needing to do anything more, let yourself enjoy the connection with this animal at whatever level it exists.*

***c*. Deepen**. *If you'd like to honor your connection with this animal more fully, open to it through your creativity. Try the following suggestions or make up your own. Before you begin, open yourself to connect more deeply by asking silently for the animal's help.*

- *Draw it in your Nature journal. Try to capture the animal's essence. Whatever the drawing actually looks like is less important than what it shows you. Give yourself free rein to tune in to your own impressions and put them on the page in whatever manner feels good to you.*

- *Dance it. Using rhythmic music without words for the background, imagine inviting the animal into your body. Then start to move — however you feel inspired. Try to let the essence of this animal come through your movements. Give yourself permission to make the animal's sounds, to act as it might. Feel how it is to be this fellow creature. Move in this way for as long as you like. How do you feel when you're dancing this animal? Is the feeling familiar? Does it remind you of some part of yourself?*

*When you've danced this animal for as long as you like, be sure to thank it for helping you, then take a moment to release it entirely from your body. Shake out all over and return to your 'normal' self.*

*Gerri chose to dance Otter:* "I've always loved to watch them down in the river. Everyone talks about how playful they are, which is true, but I'm more attracted to the quiet way they sometimes float along on their backs. It seems so peaceful. When I danced otter, though, I got so much more in touch with its active side. I just felt like twisting and twirling and really wanted to have others around me to do it with. I realized that for me otters represent the joy of companionship. I could feel it so strongly in my body! I'm making a point of calling my friends and setting up more time to be purely social. I'm thankful for the lesson."

- *Free association. Speaking aloud, repeat the phrase "This animal is …." over and over. Complete it with whatever word or words come to your mind.* "Dogs are social. Dogs are obedient. Dogs are happy to be with each other. Dogs are alert. Dogs are social. Dogs are …" *Don't worry about whether each statement makes sense literally, just speak whatever comes to your mind, then look at the general pattern that emerges.*

- *Dialog. Imagine that you could talk with this animal. What would you ask it? What might it teach you about itself or about the world of Nature? What is it here to share with you? Ask and then imagine what the answers might be. Listen carefully. What insights can this animal give you? Write them in your journal.*

*Gini enjoyed connecting with cats:* "Cat says that I need to pay more attention to my own solitude. I get angry when I have too many people around me telling me what to do. I need to show my claws from time to time, just to defend myself from all their pushing into my life. Once they understand what I mean, I won't have to keep claiming my space all the time."

***d.* Complete**. *When you've spent as much time with the animal as you'd like, complete the transaction by sharing gratitude with it. Breathe a moment to return to normal awareness, and then record anything else you learned in your Nature journal.*

# Losses

When you understand that every species of animal – as well as every tree, grass, insect, mushroom, herb, and anything else – has it's own unique place within the fabric of life, it's easy to realize that the loss of any single one will have consequences. What happens to a species of orchid, for example, when the only bat that pollinates it dies off because of insecticides sprayed on crops? What happens to a population of deer when the mountain lions that used to keep them in check are removed? What happens to the native mussels in a river when the clear water on which they depend is muddied by introduced carp? And what happens to the raccoons that feed on the mussels? What happens to a group of humans who eat mostly potatoes when those potatoes are destroyed by an introduced blight?

Of course, change is a normal part of the living world. Climate and other conditions in an area shift over time – and with them the mix of animals and plants that can live there. Just look at the fossil seashells on the highest peaks of the Rockies and the Himalayas. Usually, these changes unfold on a scale of millions of years. We live in an era, though, when human activities have enormously accelerated both the rate and the scope of environmental change. As a result, we're in the midst of what is probably the most intense period of plant and animal extinctions in the entire history of the planet.

Even as we get to know the animals around us, many of them may disappear altogether within the next few decades. You already know about the passenger pigeons, the giant mastodons, and the infamous dodo. To be honest, most of us probably get along day to day without even giving them a second thought. But where do we draw the line? Are you prepared to live in a world without elephants and rhinos and giraffes, too? Can you live without orangutans and chimps? Can you imagine a world without songbirds? In North America alone, their populations have been declining by about 10% a year. And what about butterflies? The monarchs – whose astonishing annual migration covers thousands of miles and several generations – seem to be killed by the pollen of genetically modified corn, which at this writing comprises about a third of total U.S. plantings. Every day, important links are falling out of the networks that support life on the planet. How long can that go on?

Contemplating the loss of species we love brings up difficult feelings, but our goal here isn't to upset you or make you feel guilty. Instead, let your feelings act as an incentive. Start right now, wherever you are, to connect more consciously with the plants and animals that share your world. The relationships you develop will deepen your understanding. They'll help you – and all of us – to find ways to live in greater harmony with the rest of the living world. It might not be the whole solution, but it is a good place to start.

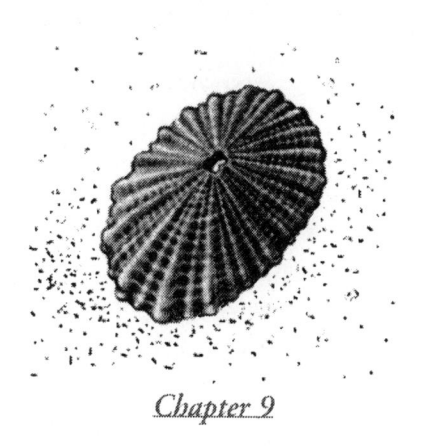

## Chapter 9

# TOPOGRAPHIES

On your first day in a new city, you'd probably make a point of buying a map to help yourself get oriented. The map, hopefully, would show you the names of streets, where they cross, and how to get around. It would give useful information about the location of parks, monuments, offices, tourist attractions, public restrooms, and maybe even postal codes. Maybe it would tell you where to catch a bus or train. With the help of your map, you'd develop a better idea of how to navigate this new territory. That's what maps are for.

Maps give us a picture of the world we live in. They show us what's important in an area and we're generally used to trusting them. In reality, though, most maps only show a relatively narrow slice of the environment. If you want to see what I mean, try bicycling through an area you usually traverse by car. Although the layout of streets and landmarks is the same, right away you'll discover other conditions your street map probably doesn't mention. Since you're depending on your own legs to get you around, suddenly you'll see hills and valleys you never noticed before. You'll discover that some streets are clogged with fast or dangerous traffic. Some have wide shoulders, while others are torn up or reek of exhaust. Although you might have noted these factors casually from the car, they take on a new immediacy from the vantage of a bike. Through the experience, you'll add new layers to the perceptual map you had before.

The same principle holds true in the realm of Nature. There are many ways to view a landscape, depending on what matters most to the person doing the viewing. If you leave the main highway, for example, your road map won't do you a lot of good. It would show most of the areas you call 'natural' as big empty spaces. Of course, you could buy maps of the hiking trails, forest roads, waterways, and so forth, but these still only go part of the way. Imagine the differences between maps of the same forest made by people with different interests. Someone who likes to fish, for example, would emphasize lakes and streams, indicating how deep they are and where to find rapids, pools, or other habitats attractive to fish. A logger, on the other hand, would be more interested in the size and types of trees, where they're found, and how accessible they are to roads. Someone who hikes might focus on areas that are scenic, quiet, and as undisturbed as possible. Of course, these three maps would overlap and some parts might be identical. Still, you get an idea of the diverse viewpoints that different people bring to the same physical terrain. Let's play with it a little and see what it's like to view your landscape in different terms.

## Experience    maps

**1. Waterways.** *Pay attention to the waterways in your area. Though they're often indicated on road maps, unless streams or rivers are especially large, they usually slip beneath our day-to-day awareness. It's easier to watch the roads and ignore the landscape they cross. Start noticing. The next time you drive across a creek, see how much you know about it. Does it have a name? Which direction does it flow? Where does it come from? What area does it drain? Where does it go?*

*Make your own map. Start with the stream or creek closest to where you live and trace its path. Where does it start? Where does it flow? Where does it pass beneath roads? How does it reach the sea? You can get most of this information from maps, but you might enjoy doing some of the initial research in person. Follow the flow of the water upstream until you find its source. Then, follow it downstream. At some point, it will join other streams and eventually a river big enough for you to follow on a map.*

*While you're thinking about it, pay attention to the water you use for drinking and household activities. When you turn on the tap, where does the water come from? Is it drawn from a well? Does it come from one of the streams you've been following? Is it local or piped in from a distance? How many other people depend on the same source? Where does your water go when you send it back down the drain? Is it purified? Does it flow back into the streams you've been mapping? Is it channeled through pipes or concrete? These bits of information are the nuts and bolts of your physical connections with the living world.*

**2. Elevation.** *Try learning some of the ups and downs of your immediate environment. Do you know how far your home is above sea level? What's the highest point in your neighborhood? And the lowest? Make a map – either mentally or in your Nature journal – and indicate the variations in elevation.*

*Pay attention to elevation, too, when you walk through your surroundings. Notice when you're going up and when you're descending. Notice whether the landscape is level or broken up. How does the world look to you from this perspective?*

3. **Distribution**. *Pick a type of plant or tree that's fairly common in your neighborhood and make a map to show its distribution. Where does this plant like to grow? Where is it densest? Does its distribution correlate to any other natural features – the way willows, for example, tend to follow streams? What other plants or animals are associated with this one and might therefore have a similar distribution?*

4. **Directions**. *Pick a place near where you live and see if you can give directions to that place without mentioning any human-made landmarks. That means no street names, no references to buildings, roads, fences, or anything else to do with people. Can you do it?*

# PERSPECTIVES

With so much variability when we consider human perspectives, imagine how much more there is when we take into account all the other creatures that share the same place. Let's play a little here. How many different ways can you see the area in which you live? Imagine looking through the eyes of a songbird, for example. How much does it matter to a migrating robin whether the fields it flies over are called 'Kentucky' or 'New York,' or whether the highway it just crossed goes to London or Timbuktu? These things – so important to human beings – are totally irrelevant to the bird. Instead, a robin might focus on how many trees are suitable for nesting or whether there are fields nearby where food is plentiful. It might consider how quiet an area is or how many cats are lurking around. It would notice – especially around nesting time – where the other robins are and know the boundaries of their territories down to the smallest twig. What a different map we'd see through the eyes of this bird!

Certainly, the worldview of a robin would include the location of earthworms. Can you imagine how one of these worms – if worms had eyes – might view the same landscape? Where is the soil rich and protected? Where is it moist? Where dry? Where has the organic content eroded away, leaving sterile gravel or clay? Where does water puddle and sit? What does a street look like to a worm trying to cross it in the rain? Even though it's the same area just mapped out by the robins, how recognizable is it?

You can take this exploration as far as you like. Think how the world looks to the squirrels, who depend on nuts and make highways of power lines and rooftops. How does it look to a pack of wolves that need large areas of undisturbed land to survive, or a flock of geese flying their V across fields and ponds in search of a safe place to spend the night? Think how the world might appear to the humpback whales who use songs to communicate over hundreds of miles. How does it look to a Golden Plover whose annual migrations between Canada and Argentina measure a distance of more than 20,000 miles? How might it look to a fish that lives in the darkness three miles beneath the surface of the ocean, or a penguin who hatches its single egg on the Antarctic ice?

They say that you can never really understand a person until you've walked a mile in their shoes. We might say that you never really know a place until you've walked – or flown, or swum, or crawled – a few miles on the wings, hooves, paws, fins, and flippers of its various inhabitants. If we can broaden our perspectives to include our companion species, we'll be able to act in ways that support the whole. Anything you can do to shift your own perspective will not only be a step in the right direction, it will also make your life that much more interesting. There's nothing to lose and much to gain.

## *Experience* PERSPECTIVES

*Here's one for your inner child. Find a natural setting that feels comfortable and welcoming, and then see how many different angles you can view it from. Once you're settled and feel aligned, move around in as many ways as you can think of. Sit in the center of the space and face outwards in different directions. Lie on the ground and look up at the sky. Face the trunk of a tree and stare at the bark. Sit in its branches and look down toward the ground. Lean your head back and look at the trees upside down. Sit in the open, beneath a bush, stand up, lie down, crouch on all fours. How do your perceptions change from place to place? How do you think the other organisms around you see this same place?*

## Experience — NIGHT WATCH

*You'd be surprised at how well your eyes really can see in the dark. It just takes a while – ten to twenty minutes – for them to adjust. Why not try it? On a night with no moon, go to a natural place that feels safe and welcoming. The less artificial light around you the better. It might be best to go somewhere you're already familiar with, rather than somewhere brand new. Once you're there, find a spot to sit quietly and turn off your flashlight. Then, just sit and wait.*

*While your eyes are adjusting to the darkness, center your mind by following your breath. Tune in by using your senses other than vision. How are the sounds at night? Are they different from what you're used to hearing in the day? How aware are you of smells? Are you more aware of the textures within reach of your hands? Notice how this experience compares to what you're accustomed to during the daytime.*

*Are you aware of any animals around you? Often, those that are active at night are entirely different from those in the same place during the day. Extend your awareness outward and see what you notice.*

*What feelings does this process bring up? Do those feelings change as your vision adjusts and you start to get more information through your eyes? How is your night vision different from your day vision? How would you describe the experience?*

*When you've stayed in this place as long as you like, thank it for sharing with you. Turn on your light and return home. Record your impressions in your Nature journal.*

## Experience — BEAUTY WALK

*Whatever we're looking for in the world is what we tend to see. It's all a matter of focus. Here's a chance to explore how your intention can affect your view of the world. Enjoy it.*

## CONNECTING WITH NATURE                                         75

*a.* **Beauty**. *Take a walk in a welcoming natural setting. As you set out, ask yourself to focus on 'beauty.' Ask your eyes, your ears, all your senses to show you the beauty in this place; then just walk. As you do, repeat this request over and over in your mind: "Show me the beauty. Show me the beauty. Show me..." Then, see what you notice.*

*It's fascinating how different people hiking through the same area will notice different things. Here's what a few people said who went on the same hike:*

*Jim commented:* "The shapes of the leaves are so wonderful! Just like snowflakes, no two exactly alike."

*Betty observed:* "When the wind rustles the trees, the patches of sunlight moving around on the forest floor look like water."

*Sally said:* "The little orange mushrooms under the hickory tree caught my eye."

*Brad added:* "I noticed how the mosses on the gray rocks look like a whole miniature landscape."

*Witnessing the beauty of the natural world is not only one of the best ways to honor it – it's also very good practice for the rest of your life. Can you do the same thing with other people? Can you do it with the animals and plants around you? Can you practice it as you look at yourself?*

*b.* **Open to the world.** *Once you've explored 'beauty,' try the same experience again and change your focus. Try to notice 'flowers.' Pay attention to 'textures.' Make up your own topics – connection, recycling, family, cooperation, oneness, sharing, wonder, movement – whatever you like. See how your perceptions change each time. When you're finished, thank the environment. Record what you notice in your Nature journal.*

### *Experience*     DIRECTIONS

*Many animals have a sense of direction strong enough to guide them over long journeys with few landmarks. Humans have the same ability, although most of us tend to forget. Many traditional peoples have held the cardinal directions (north, east, south, and west) to be so important that they've developed detailed descriptions of the energetic qualities associated with each one. Details vary, but many of these descriptions draw on symbolic meanings related to the movement of the sun and the passage of the seasons.*

*Briefly, east is often associated with the active, expansive energy of new beginnings – sunrise, springtime, a new relationship, or the start of any endeavor. South (at least in the northern hemisphere) is the place of coming into fullness – mid-day, mid-summer, the ripening of relationship, or the fruition of an activity. In the west, the cycle begins to shift as energies contract and thoughts turn inward – end of day, autumn harvest, or any time of introspection and completion. Finally, north holds the quiet time of reflection and planning before a new cycle begins – night, winter, or the time of sleep, rest, and recharging.*

*How much are the directions a part of your life? Do you know which direction your house faces? Do you know where the sun rises and where the moon sets? Can you tell which direction you're facing when you're outdoors? Do you know which direction you're facing right now, as you read these words?*

*Sit at sunrise, mid-day, or sunset and spend a few minutes facing east, south, west, and north. How do you feel when you contemplate each of the four directions? Do you notice any difference from one to another? Is one more comfortable than the others? Do you think there's a real energy associated with these directions? If so, can you describe it?*

*Make the directions a part of your everyday awareness. Which direction do you drive when you go from your house to the store? In which do you go when you leave work? When you go to a friend's? When you return home later? Pay attention and see if anything changes.*

*Chapter 10*

# FROM THE GROUND UP

A few miles from my home stands a huge granite outcrop called Stone Mountain. It's a popular tourist attraction, complete with an enormous military carving on the side, an artificial lake, a faux steamboat, and tons of Civil War memorabilia. I like to visit the park a few times a year, but I don't go for the attractions. I visit because what grows on the mountain is fascinating. When you stand at the top, your first glace shows a landscape that seems totally barren. When you look more closely, though, you see that a thin veneer of life has colonized the bare granite. Patches of pale green lichen cling to the gray rock like living stains. In depressions where enough gravel has collected to hold a little moisture, plants so tiny you have to bend down to see them cling to life. Farther down the slope, a thin layer of soil supports green 'islands' that include moss, grasses, shrubs, and even a few scrubby pine trees whose roots grab a foothold in whatever cracks they can find.

I love to sit at the edge of these islands, where a low green wall of moss suddenly interrupts the bare stone. The contrast between the rock and the living plants beside it is striking. It accentuates just how tenuous a hold these patches of life actually have. Every few years, lightning or a cigarette starts a fire that reduces one of them to a patch of charred sticks. Occasionally, a strong wind pushes over one of the trees, turning up a root system just a few inches deep. But the living organisms here are also tenacious. Within a few weeks after a fire, patches of green push their way up through the charred soil. Even before a fallen tree dies, new growth starts to re-colonize the spot it once held. Watching, it's difficult not to be awed as life on the mountain mirrors in miniature the processes that occur on a much greater scale around the whole planet.

If you could look at the Earth in cross section, right away you'd notice how small a part of it actually supports life. What seems to us to be a huge and inexhaustible realm of forests, plains, and grasslands is in fact quite delicate. From this view, all of that life looks like an impossibly thin covering that has wrapped itself by root and tendril around a barren, rocky planet. Much of its success depends on the capacity of the smallest organisms to transform inert ingredients – rock, gravel, and minerals – into the vital topsoil that supports all the rest of terrestrial life.

Topsoil is a complex and dynamic substance. Its core is a mix of stones, gravel, sand, and clay that have broken down from the underlying rock. Around the inorganic particles, a mass of organic matter called 'humus' – a combination of rotting wood, leaves, animal remains, and so forth – adds nutrients and helps hold the water and air necessary to support life. The rest of the soil is a large, interdependent community of algae, fungi, bacteria, and other microorganisms. These creatures are responsible for a complicated set of chemical processes that provide nutrients for higher plants – including gathering and storing minerals as well as the all-important job of breaking down and recycling organic materials. In many ways, soil acts as the binder that holds all the other parts of the ecosystem together. If the rocks are the grandfathers that give rise to all life, then the soil is the means by which they do so.

Any traditional farmer will tell you that mature, healthy topsoil is a treasure not to be taken for granted. It takes a very long time to form – something like 500 years per inch – and if left unprotected can be lost in the blink of an eye. Unfortunately, each year we lose enormous amounts of topsoil worldwide, because of poor farming practices, over-development, deforestation, overgrazing, drought, and other factors. Indeed, deserts are advancing at an unprecedented rate, threatening as much as a third of the planet's ice-free land. Even the highly touted productivity of 'modern' agriculture, with its mammoth inputs of petroleum-based fertilizers and other chemicals, hasn't altered the fact that our long-term survival depends on keeping the soil we have.

Soil is the rich underside of the rest of life. Appreciating it intellectually is a good start, but to really understand it, you've got to get down and dirty. My own education in this realm started the day I built my first compost pile. Have you ever seen one? A compost pile is basically a domesticated version of the soil that lives all around us. At my house, it lives in a shady spot in the back yard. We feed it clippings from the garden, scraps from the kitchen, and leaves and other debris from the yard. These all get covered by a thin layer of earth, dug from somewhere else in the pile. Whenever we dig into the pile, the shovel exposes a mass of hungry worms, grubs, and other critters. White threads of fungus weave through the parts around the edges. On summer nights, a blanket of crickets, beetles, and an occasional opossum often covers it. There's rarely any odor, except the fragrance of moist earth, and when it really gets cooking, the pile creates its own warmth. Several years ago, I read an article about how to use the heat from a large compost pile to cook a carefully wrapped Thanksgiving turkey. Talk about hard core!

Just like any other member of the family, the compost pile depends on a regular supply of food, water, and air. If it misses any one of these, the community of organisms that keeps it functioning dies off and the pile stops working. As long as we take care of it, though, the pile's ability to digest is remarkable. All the organic wastes we put into it – most of which would have otherwise been lugged to the curb and hauled to the landfill – disappear amazingly quickly. What appears in their place is a rich dark loam that acts like magic in the garden. Indeed, the process is so satisfying that almost everyone I know who keeps a compost pile gets really attached to it. We make up a sort of underground society, exchanging tips and stories with each other when nobody else is around. I've known 'composters' who carried buckets of their old pile with them when they moved, just to have 'starter' for the new yard. Others complain of how appalled they are to dine with friends who don't compost. "The amount of garbage they throw away! All that good material just wasted." Do you think that's extreme? If you've never kept a compost pile, then probably so. However, if you've had or have one, you'll understand. Welcome to the club.

How about you? Are you ready to dig in the soil?

## *Experience*     GET YOUR HANDS DIRTY

*a.* **Investigate**. *Do a little detective work about the soil in your neighborhood. First, if you can, find an area that's either wooded or relatively undisturbed. Make sure it feels welcoming to you. Then, with a small trowel or shovel, dig a few inches into the topsoil and observe what it's like. What makes up the very top layer? Is there a covering of leaves or vegetation to help keep it from washing away? How about farther down? What color is the soil here? What texture does it have? How moist is it? How does it change from the surface downward? How many different organisms can you observe just in this small sample? If your soil is healthy, the vast majority of organisms will be too small to see with the naked eye.*

*Notice as much as you can about the soil. Record your findings in your Nature journal, if you like, then replace the soil (with gratitude) when you're finished. Be sure to replace the covering of leaves or vegetation so you leave the spot as close to the way you found it as possible.*

*b.* **Compare**. *Repeat the same soil investigation in other places. Look at the soil in a lawn, for example, or a garden. See what it's like where the land has been bulldozed or disturbed by construction. Look at it in a site where there's been a lot of erosion. What do you notice? How does the soil differ from place to place? Do you see any correlations between the character of the soil and the plants that are growing in it? Can you see any association between the amount of plant cover and other conditions in the soil? What else do you notice?*

## *Experience*    BAREFOOT

*Funny, isn't it, how shoes and civilization seem to go together. Shoes protect our feet, to be sure, but they also close us off from a lot of information. If you're used to wearing shoes all the time, try walking barefoot for a while in a safe natural place. What can your feet tell you? Notice the texture of the ground beneath you. Notice the changes in temperature from one place to another. Notice how having your feet directly on the Earth affects your balance. 'Listen' with your feet. What do they tell you when you're walking on stones, on sand, on leaves, in mud, through a stream? What textures do you like the best? Which is more challenging? What else do you notice?*

# COOPERATION

Soil is one of the foundations of the living world. When I'm sitting on Stone Mountain, though, sometimes my thoughts turn toward a different sort of foundation – cooperation. Many of us, if we thought about it at all, grew up with an image of the natural world as a hotbed of intense competition. Tennyson's description of "Nature, red in tooth and claw" has become popularized shorthand for the complexities of evolutionary theory – and also a misguided justification for a good many shortsighted human activities. Competition is one way that living organisms interact – but it's far from the only one. Let's change our lens for a moment and see from a different perspective.

We could start right here on the mountain, with the lichens. Lichens represent a highly evolved partnership between fungus and algae, a form of cooperation that offers distinct benefits to both. The fungus provides the outer structure that adheres to the surface of the rock and also absorbs water and nutrients. The algae live within the fungus and contribute nutritional compounds derived from photosynthesis. Together, these partners are widely successful, occupying habitats as inhospitable as rock, the bark of trees, and bare ground in the far reaches of the Arctic. On Stone Mountain, lichen helps anchor particles of sand and debris to create a rudimentary soil that gives other organisms a foothold. Here, it's usually mosses, which in turn hold more soil until larger plants and eventually trees take over. At each step of the process, the various organisms work together to create the conditions that allow them all to survive.

If you look around the realm of Nature, you can see lots of other examples. Look at squirrels and oaks. The squirrels hide acorns beneath the soil, effectively planting the trees that provide them with both food and shelter. Look at how many 'extra' acorns the trees produce each year – providing for squirrels and other animals in the process of ensuring their own continuing survival. Consider the relationship between ants and aphids. Aphids are small insects that feed on the juices of plants. Ants move them from place to place and protect them from predators. When stroked by the ants, the aphids secrete drops of sweet juice that provide their caretakers with food.

Sometimes, the relationships are even more intimate. Termites depend entirely on the microorganisms in their digestive tracts to break down the wood they consume. We humans harbor an enormous population of bacteria in our own intestines, which among other things produce several essential vitamins. Different bacteria associated with the roots of plants take nitrogen from the atmosphere and make it available to other organisms – a task so vital to life that if these bacteria suddenly disappeared, no other plant or animal on the planet would survive. At an even more fundamental level, it's very likely that ancient cooperation between different single-celled organisms was responsible for the development of all the multicellular plants and animals alive today.

Living systems are multifaceted and complex. No single mechanism – whether cooperation, competition, or anything else – governs the interactions between organisms all by itself. Instead, all these factors work together in ways that ultimately support the functioning of the whole system. In the soil, for example, or a compost pile, you'll find a multitude of individual spe-

# CONNECTING WITH NATURE                                              83

cies. As each one competes for its share of the available resources, the entire assemblage effectively works together to perpetuate the survival of the whole. Among populations of larger animals, look at the balance between predators and their prey. While being eaten by a mountain lion isn't the most positive experience for an individual deer, the fact that natural predators tend to remove weak or sick individuals helps to promote the overall health of both species. Individual trees in a forest may compete for space and sunlight, yet the fact that they all live together creates conditions – higher soil moisture, greater resistance to winds, and a concentration of nutrients – that tend to benefit them all.

From now on, when you look at the more visible parts of the natural world, keep in mind their less visible partners. Remember what holds the system together. Remember who keeps the trees, plants, and larger animals healthy. Just as adding compost will enrich the soil of your garden, your awareness of these foundations will enrich your own appreciation of the living world. Remember your roots!

## *Experience*     INTERACTIONS

> *Think of a tree, green plant, or animal that feels special to you. Write its name in the center of a new page in your Nature journal. Then, see how many other organisms you can think of that interact with the first one. Write their names around the name of your chosen organism. Indicate the nature of the relationship by drawing an arrow toward the one who benefits directly from the exchange. If both benefit, make an arrow pointing in both directions.*
>
> *For example: Say you've chosen the maple tree in your back yard. Write 'maple' or make a small picture of the tree in the center of your page. Then, think what that tree might interact with. You know there's a pair of doves that nested there last year. Write (or draw a) 'dove' somewhere on the page. Since the tree benefits the doves, without a lot of apparent benefit in return, make an arrow in that direction. You've seen a chipmunk that likes to collect the maple seeds in the springtime, so indicate that with a differ-*

*ent arrow, toward the chipmunk. Beneath the tree, earthworms live in the soil. They seem to thrive in the shade created by the tree and also aerate the soil so it soaks up more moisture during a rain. Indicate the worms and draw an arrow in both directions.*

*Continue brainstorming until you've come up with as many connections as you can. When you've finished, you'll have created a generalized diagram of the network of interconnections around your maple tree. What does it show you?*

*Could you imagine a similar diagram with yourself in the center? What would your connections look like?*

## Experience    GARBAGE

*In the natural world, nothing ever goes to waste. Anything discarded by one organism becomes food for another. Anything that falls to the ground is broken down in the soil – feeding the microorganisms that live there and freeing up nutrients for all the rest. In a natural system, there is nothing that isn't reduced, recycled, or reused.*

*What about in your life? Do you know where your trash goes? When you put it out to be collected, what happens to the food scraps? What happens to the cans, the bottles, and the paper? What happens to old pieces of lumber, cardboard boxes, or all the various kinds of plastic? Are any of these items recycled? Are any of the reusable parts saved? Where does the rest go? Is it incinerated? Buried? Dumped? Where?*

*Ask a few questions. Find out where the trash from your community goes. Is there a recycling program where you live? If so, how effective do you think it is? Could you think of a way to make it better? If there isn't one, is there any way to create one?*

## Experience    COMPOST

*For a long-term experience that will help you put your own roots back into the soil, why not consider starting your own compost pile. Of course, you'll need a place to put it. If you've got a yard, that's great. If not, consider sharing the process with a friend who does, or working through a community garden.*

*Although composting is relatively simple, there are many ways to proceed and a broad range of opinions regarding which techniques work best. How you proceed will necessarily depend on where you live and the conditions around you. To learn where to start in your area, do a little research. The best source for practical advice would probably be other gardeners who have direct experience. Beyond that, you can get information from books, extension services, the library, and many different sites on the internet.*

*Composting, like gardening, is a learning process. You probably don't need a lot of expensive equipment to start off – though it's out there if you want to buy it. Start as simply as possible and see what happens. If you're not happy with the results of your initial experiment, then figure out how you might improve your process. Once you get it going, your compost pile will be an easy, ongoing, and productive part of your own connection with the living world.*

*Chapter 11*

# GAIA

In late summer, my garden is host to a sudden cloud of speckled orange butterflies called fritillaries. They flutter around in pairs and trios, covering the whole terrain, but always returning to the corner by the passionflower vines. Passionflowers are where female fritillaries lay their bright yellow eggs. If you look carefully, you can see them beneath the leaves. In a few weeks, the vines are covered with voracious, hairy caterpillars and after that, more butterflies. Most years, I get very few of the elaborate purple and white flowers; instead, I get fritillaries. It's a fair trade. I don't mind growing butterflies. Elsewhere in the garden, honeybees pollinate the sweet peas and hummingbirds visit the orange trumpet flowers. Woodpeckers keep the magnolia free of bark-boring beetles. Yellow and black zebra spiders feast on flies and birds feast on them. All around the garden – and everywhere else in Nature – are connections on top of connections on top of connections. In fact, you could search your entire lifetime and never find a single organism that lives without being connected to many, many others.

Up to this point in our exploration, we've looked at various aspects of the living world one at a time. That's a good way to focus on their individual characteristics, yet if we stop there, we miss a vital part of the picture. None of these pieces could exist without the others. To really understand Nature, we need to look at how all the different parts interconnect to make a whole system. None of us are separate here. Trees, humans, whales, roaches, butterflies, passionflowers, and every other living creature are inseparably and inextricably part of the same great planet.

At one level, the idea that we're all part of the Earth might seem self-evident. Of course we are. Unfortunately, though, we don't always act that way. However good our intentions, our actions get undermined by that same insidious belief that humans are separate from the rest of Nature. No matter that we really know better, society still reinforces that old attitude in many ways. You see it in the story that the first humans were expelled from the primeval garden. You see it in the attitude – whether stated or implied – that our technology somehow frees us from the rules governing the rest of life. It's there in the belief that someone gave us the right to treat every other living creature as a resource to be 'managed' for our own benefit. It's implied in all the action film fantasies that some superhero will arrive just in the nick of time, or that we can vault off to the stars if we mess up here. In fact, all these swirling ideas prop up a premise that is inherently false. We humans are no more separate from the rest of the living planet than your own liver cells are separate from you.

The oneness of all life is beautifully enunciated in the stories of many different peoples. Most of these include the concept of the Earth as mother – or father – of all life. The name itself, Earth, derives from the name the tribes of northern Germany once gave the mother goddess. The Sumerians named her Ninhursag-ki, the one whose womb pushes forth all precious things. Among the ancient Chinese as well as many Native American peoples, the Earth was seen as a giant turtle whose shell either supported or contained all living beings. The Egyptians honored a male deity, Geb, who gave rise to all vegetation. The Greeks worshipped Gaia, the goddess of Earth, whose body brought forth plants, animals, and all the rest of creation.

In the 1970's, James Lovelock and Lynn Margulis reintroduced Gaia to Western science. As part of a NASA project to determine chemical characteristics that might indicate the presence of life on other planets, they observed that the Earth acts in many ways as a single, self-regulating system. They noticed that a number of atmospheric factors – oxygen and carbon dioxide levels, temperature, and others – act as if some regulatory mechanism were keeping them within the very narrow range of values that supports life. Their 'Gaia hypothesis' was a powerful call for scientists to change long-held perspectives and view the planet as a single living whole. Although it remains controversial in some circles, the idea has gained widespread popular recognition as the basis for a healthier worldview. For many people, it puts into words something they've known intuitively all along.

Whether or not you take the Gaia hypothesis literally, remember that 'hypothesis' doesn't mean a proven fact, but rather a question to be examined. Yet what if it were true? What if we did view the Earth as a living creature? Let's look at what that might mean to our concept of ourselves and our relationship with Nature.

- If everything is connected, relationship is vital. In your body, you could spend years studying just the cells of your heart. You'd learn that they respond to electrical pulses, start beating long before birth, and respond strongly to minerals like sodium and potassium. In the environment, you could look at a maple tree and learn how its roots bring in water, why its leaves fall in response to day length, and how its seeds form in response to pollination by the wind. All these facts are interesting and important, yet their full significance is only clear when you consider their greater context. Neither heart cells nor maple trees can live apart from the bigger systems that contain them – your body in the first case, the forest or the Earth in the second. To understand the real picture, we need to ask how each part functions within the whole. How does it affect the individuals around it? How does it support the well-being of the system it lives in?

- Every part has its own place within the whole. In your body, there are something like ten trillion individual cells, divided into hundreds of different types. Each group of cells has its own important job. If any one type were to malfunction, say the cells of your pancreas or thyroid, you can see that the whole body would be affected. On a larger scale, the total number of species on Earth is estimated at between five to twenty million different organisms. Can you recognize that each one of these, from elephants to amoebas, also makes its own important contributions to the health of the planet? We've looked at some of the more obvious contributions already – green plants store sunlight, trees provide us with oxygen, certain bacteria supply us all with the nitrogen we need. Even though we may not understand the exact role of every species, each one has its place.

- Everything we have is shared. If the Earth is a living organism, what are the 'natural resources' around us? Take water. Only about one percent of all the water on the planet is fresh enough to drink, and that's all we have to supply the needs of every tree, animal, plant, and human (and of course compost pile) on land – not to mention all the industrial uses we put it to. Already, we use well over half of what's available and shortages are becoming severe in many parts of the world. How much water does that leave for the other organisms? What happens when we run out? Can one cell within a body justify taking all the blood from those around it?

    What if we take the perspective of Gaia. How would we treat the water, for example, if we knew it as our own blood pouring from the faucet? How would we act if we really knew, in our heart of hearts, the mountains to be our bones, the trees our lungs, the soil the skin of our own great body? How would we act if we recognized the animals as our brothers and sisters, the plants as our own flesh, the air as the breath that all of us share? How would we see these things we still call 'resources?' How, in the end, would we see ourselves?

- The Earth's health is our health. It makes no sense to separate the parts from the whole, whether in your body or that of the planet. How can we talk about 'healthy' brain cells, for example, if the rest of the body is riddled with cancer? How can we protect baby sea turtles, say, without also addressing the fact that the oceans we're releasing them into are sour with pollution?

The health of the individual depends on the health of the whole.

At an individual level, of course, nothing lives forever. In your body, cells die all the time. As long as strong new ones replace weak and damaged ones, you stay healthy. But what happens to your health if cells start dying faster than they're replaced? In our planetary body, the rate at which we're losing entire species could be as high as 50,000 per year. If present trends continue, we could lose *half* the world's species within the next century. How do you think that will affect the health of the planet? How do you think it will affect the health of humanity?

Ultimately, we're all in this together – sink, swim, or learn to fly. One of the most important things we can do right now is awaken to a new vision of this living Earth. No matter how engrained the old habits, there's no way to avoid the basic truth. Human beings cannot live without the other species on the planet. We can never be truly healthy, neither as individuals nor as a species, until our planetary body is also healthy. By raising our sights and looking at the world from Gaia's perspective, we take the necessary step towards a revolutionary change.

I'll tell you a secret. Once you recognize that you have a place within this living being we call Earth, you'll be surprised at the depth of comfort the idea brings. Yes, there are challenges. Yes, there's a lot of work to do. Yet there is also incredible support. We're not here alone. As individuals and as part of humanity, each one of us is part of this beautiful living jewel of a planet. Just as every cell in your body contains the genetic information to create any other, so too you contain the wonders of the entire planet within your being. In your cells resonate the heights of the Himalayas, the breadth of the Amazon, the stark glory of an Antarctic sunrise. In your cells, you are one with redwoods, dolphins, wolves, eagles, and duck-billed platypuses. Everything that life is, you are. Every place that life unfolds its multicolored glory, there you are, too. Step beyond yourself for a moment and open to this new way of seeing. The step you take will bring you the world.

## Experience   CONNECTIONS

**a. Interactions.** *Pick any organism and do a little brainstorming. What beneficial relationships can you find between this organism and others around it? If you were to outline this creature's contributions to the well-being of Gaia, what might they be? Think of how a hummingbird carries pollen from flower to flower. Think about how the flowers feed the hummingbird. Think about how the sunshine helps them both. Find as many connections as you can.*

*If you choose, you can reach the same place from the opposite direction. What would change if this organism were no longer here? If these oaks disappeared, how many different organisms would be affected? Squirrels. Soil. Shrubs. Fungus. Worms. Nesting birds. Grubs that live beneath the bark and the woodpeckers that live on them. If you held a funeral for that departed organism, who would show up?*

*Play with your imagination here and try to expand your sense of possibility. Of course, the contributions of many organisms might be hard to perceive right away. See what you can come up with. Enjoy being creative as you look at the world from a systems perspective.*

**b. Your place.** *Think about yourself as a 'cell' within this living Earth. What's your job here? Where do you receive support from the other 'cells' around you? How do you support them? What materials do you share with each other? How are you a part of the larger phenomena – weather, seasons, landscape, water cycles, etc – that you observe around yourself? How many different species do you affect?*

*Take your time and outline some of your major interconnections within this living planet.*


## Experience   ATTRACTION

**a. Attractions.** *Sit quietly in a welcoming natural setting. Focus on your breath as a way to tune in to yourself and your surroundings. When you feel centered, ask yourself, "What attracts me here?" Look around. Notice how you feel as you contemplate each part of your surroundings. Which* *parts feel most positive? Which draw you more than others? If you like, make a list in your journal.*

The color of the leaves is really pleasing.

I want to sit in the shade – I just feel better there.

The willow tree in the corner is beautiful. I like to just watch it.

Anywhere I can feel the breeze is really nice.

*Notice the quality of these attractions. What do they feel like? Where do you feel them in your body? Are they the same as or different from the attractions you feel in other areas of your life?*

***b.* Map**. *Sketch a diagram of the major attractions you feel in this area. If you want, draw them as lines that go from you to the various parts of your surroundings.*

*The urge to connect is deeply engrained in each one of us – but what do you think happens on the other side of the equation? Do you think the natural world feels the same urge to connect as you do? Is there a chance that the attraction you're feeling could actually be mutual? Based on your experience with people, pets, or other creatures, what do you think?*

*Reflect on what parts of the environment might be attractive to the various organisms around you. How, for example, might a patch of thick, leafy shrubs appear to a bird seeking a place to roost for the night? What might a thirsty deer feel about a pool of clear water? Imagine adding to the map of attractions you just drew for yourself all the attractions felt by the other organisms around you. How far do you think it might go? What role do you think attraction plays within the body of Gaia?*

***c.* Repulsion**. *The other side of attraction is repulsion. Some parts of your environment are less attractive than others. Look around you. Which aspects of your immediate surroundings seem less inviting? List them. Pay attention to your body. Where inside you does the feeling of repulsion exist? Can you describe it? Do you think there's a reason? Is there any sort of message that is communicated by the feeling?*

*Think about where you've felt this sort of feeling in the past. Think about some of the things that are repellent to almost everyone, like the smell of spoiled food or bodily waste. Do you think there's a reason? When you think that these very same fragrances might be highly attractive to other organisms (flies, for example), what might that say about the way things work in the natural world?*

*Here's food for thought. Do you think there might be some sort of inborn mechanism that steers you towards situations or environments that are more positive to you and away from others that aren't? Think about it.*

## *Experience*     PERMEABLE BOUNDARIES

*There's a lot more going on in the world than generally meets the eye. Along with the senses like vision and hearing that are familiar to all of us, we can also gather information via other faculties that are generally less well known. One of these is the ability to sense energy.*

*Energy is a universal quality that infuses everything in the material world. There are many ways to name and describe it. When we're talking about living beings, we could call this energy 'aura,' 'vital force,' or 'chi.' Learning to sense, manipulate, and balance it is an important aspect of traditional healing systems around the planet.*

*Every person is capable of sensing energy. You probably feel it already, although you might not be conscious of doing so. If the concept is new to you, it might seem strange or fanciful, but in reality it is tangible and quite practical. Most people can feel energy quite easily. The following experience will give you a short introduction. We'll start by tuning in to the energy of your own body.*

***a.* Hands**. *Sit quietly and comfortably, and then rub your hands together lightly and briskly. When they feel warm, hold them a few inches apart, with the palms facing toward each other. Keep your shoulders and arms relaxed. Put your attention into the palms of your hands and notice what you feel there. You may notice a slight sensation of tingling, warmth, coolness, or density. Stay relaxed and observe. Everyone senses energy differently. If you stay focused, very soon you'll find your own way.*

*Once you start to sense something, however faintly, slowly and gently move your hands farther apart and closer together. Do you notice any changes? People often report that the warmth or tingling in their hands increases or decreases as they move them. Some say that their hands feel like magnets, gently attracting or repelling each other.*

*What you're sensing is very subtle. You may need some time to get used to it. If you're not feeling anything yet, relax and be patient. Usually, a little practice is all it takes. Be sure your body is relaxed, that you're breathing gently, and that your hands are fairly close together. In a short time, you'll probably find that this is simple and easy.*

**b. Sharpen**. *When you begin to notice some sort of sensation in your hands, deepen your experience by trying to describe it. Though none of the following terms may be accurate literally, they'll help you hone your energy-sensing skill. While you pay attention to the feelings between your hands, ask yourself the following questions:*

- *If I could see the energy, what color would it be?*
- *What 'texture' does it have? Is it 'dense' or 'light?'*
- *Is it hot, cool, warm, cold?*
- *Is it static? Does it pulse?*
- *Does it seem to move in a certain direction?*
- *What else do I notice about this energy?*

**c. Tree**. *Experiment with feeling the energy of various things around you. One of the easiest ways to begin is with a tree. Rub your hands together, and then bring your palms slowly closer to the trunk. You'll probably notice a change in sensation as they get closer. When you do, keep your hands steady and ask yourself the questions from part b. Then, bring your hands all the way to the trunk and hold them there lightly. Notice what you feel as you do so.*

**d. Environment**. *Try the same procedure with other things:*

- *a stone or rock*
- *a table, chair, or other piece of furniture*

- *a houseplant*
- *an apple, banana, or other type of food*
- *a cat, dog, or other small animal*
- *whatever else calls you*

*What do you notice? Are you able to feel the energy? Can you notice differences from object to object? If you were able to experience the energy easily, continue to explore the world around you in this way.*

*When you consider that everything in the world has an energetic body, what does that suggest about the ways that we connect with each other?*

*Chapter 12*

# HUMANITY AND NATURE

Within this great being we call Gaia, everyone and everything has its own role to play. So far, we've looked at how a number of organisms fulfill theirs. Trees produce oxygen. Earthworms enrich and aerate the soil. Bacteria help everyone, from termites to cows, from aardvarks to humans, to digest their dinners. Plants harvest sunlight. Deer, lions, and lichens all have their places, too, within the greater body of life. We've looked all around us, yet up to this point we've only touched briefly on what is probably the most important question of all – what are we here for? Ever since humanity first appeared on the scene, we've had a major effect on the species and the landscapes around us. Over the centuries – especially within the past hundred years – we've grown to such an extent that our actions effectively dominate every part of the entire system. Now, more than ever, we need to look in the mirror and ask: "What is humanity's role within the living planet?"

As you might expect, we're not the first to ask. From the beginning of time, people have reflected on the same question. As you've seen, many of the answers provided by our Western intellectual tradition have been built upon the premise of separation between humanity and everybody else. One interesting alternative was presented in the mid-1900's by a French philosopher named Pierre Teilhard de Chardin.

Decades before the Gaia hypothesis, Teilhard suggested that part of humanity's purpose might be to act as a sort of global brain, the physical embodiment of a growing planetary consciousness. Since then, the image of humanity as the brains of the planet has become widely popular. You hear it frequently in discussions of global communications. The phones, TV's, radios, computers, and other hardware of the network are likened to nerve cells and the network they create is touted as the start of an era of global unity and freedom. Unfortunately, so far the hype is stronger that the results. Although it is a step in the right direction, the global communication system can only reflect the ideas and beliefs of the people who use it. Until we change our collective focus, it will probably continue to reinforce the same old separation.

The society we live in tends to value the mind above all else. Indeed, one of the main criteria generally used to distinguish us from other living beings is our 'superior' mental capacity. Yet if we define ourselves – and our role on the planet – solely in terms of our mental capabilities, we sell ourselves far short of our true potential. We are more than our minds; we have bodies and hearts and deep spiritual sensibilities. The same impulse that separates us from Nature also tends to cut us off from the fullness of our own beings. The resulting alienation affects us deeply.

Psychologically, this alienation can manifest as a fear that everything 'out there' – from mosquitoes to our own impulses – is out to get us, or as a sort of 'every man for himself' competitiveness that undermines community and stresses our health. Emotionally, it might show up as a deep sadness about the state of the Earth or a sense of overwhelm when we think about trying to improve it. Spiritually, it can feed the profound loneliness and desperate search for meaning that underlies much of society's frantic busyness. If we believe we're isolated from everything we see, what's the point of being here? If we don't belong here, where do we belong? How can we contribute to the greater-good if we think that the rest of creation has no significance?

The time to move from separation to connection is now. How do you do that? Actually, you already are, each time you focus on the living world and your place within it. You shift each time you step beyond old ways of seeing and really feel the depth of your own connection with Nature. To shift even more fully, turn your connection with the living world into a regular, ongoing part of your life.

Earth-based societies have long understood the vital importance of remembering where we are and how we fit into the greater whole. Most of these societies developed regular cycles of ritual and ceremony to mark important events and to promote balance within the world. Though the form of these celebrations varies widely from people to people, the intentions behind them are remarkably constant – to honor life, to remind ourselves of our place within the whole, and to 'feed' the world by giving something back. They promote a fundamental change of perspective. Instead of demanding, "What can the world give to me?" they ask, "What can I give to the world?" You can use the same principles to create your own practice of intentional connection.

Practicing intentional connection is simple, effective, and highly personalized. All it involves is taking time to honor those parts of the living world that touch you most deeply. Choose events and relationships that have meaning for you, no matter what they mean to anyone else. A good place to start – and the core of many traditional systems – is to honor the basic rhythms of life and planet. You might…

- observe the sunrise and the sunset.
- mark the phases of the moon and the passage of the seasons.
- mark your birthday, your entry into this great extended family.
- honor significant events in your life and the lives of the people you love. Every society on the planet has developed rituals to mark births, deaths, partnership, and the passages from child to adolescent, adolescent to adult, adult to elder.
- offer your thanks for the important relationships in your life – with other people, with special places, with plants and animals.
- share your gratitude for the organisms who give their lives so that you can eat.
- take a moment to appreciate those that make your environment

beautiful or hospitable.
- witness the beauty that feeds you each day.
- honor whatever brings you joy, health, support, and inspiration.

How do you start? First, decide what you want to honor. Then, create a simple, personal ritual that helps you to do so. In this context, a ritual is any series of words or actions that helps you to communicate your heart-felt intention to connect with the living world. It can be as simple or as elaborate as you like. Although you're free to incorporate elements from any religious tradition that speaks to you, the rituals you create for yourself could be entirely secular. The only thing that matters is that your ritual be meaningful for you.

## *Experience*   INTENTIONAL CONNECTION

*Use the following guidelines to design a simple, personal ritual to honor your own connection with the living world. As you move through the steps, think about what you'd like to honor and how you might proceed.*

***a.* Set your intention**. *Focused intention is what sets ritual actions apart from normal, day-to-day activities. To begin, choose a simple action to indicate that you intend to focus your full attention on whatever follows. It could be a short prayer — especially if you follow a religious tradition — or an invitation to the energies of spirit to join you. It might be a simple gesture like reaching down to touch the Earth, turning to each of the four cardinal directions, or taking three slow, deep breaths. You could light a candle, sing, ring a small bell, touch your heart, or whatever else feels right to you.*

*Setting your intention establishes the tone for your whole ritual. It reminds you that you're creating a space that is special, outside the flow of normal activity. You'll find that the more you repeat a certain opening gesture, the more comforting and familiar it becomes. In time, just repeating it will help you calm your mind and focus your attention quickly and easily.*

***b.* Communicate**. *When you've opened your ritual, how you proceed depends on your intention. What are you here to honor? What would you like to express? The possibilities are endless — and entirely up to you.*

*Susan likes to convey what she's feeling with words*: "I go into the woods about once a week and sit with my back to one of the trees. I start by singing a long tone, then wait till I feel centered. Then, I just talk. I give thanks for the people in my life. I give thanks to the trees, the flowers, and the animals. If there's a problem I'm dealing with, I ask for help. Mostly, though, I just say thanks to the world around me. If I get busy and forget to go for a while, I miss it."

*Jenny goes to the ocean to witness the full moon:* "I stand on the beach right after sunset. I usually take a few flowers as a little offering. Then, I just breathe as consciously as I can while the moon comes up over the water. The beauty of it always makes me feel glad to be alive. I go even when it's rainy or cloudy, just to be there."

*Each year, when Bill sees the first flower in his garden, he brings it inside and floats it in a little bowl on the mantle.* "My whole family comes in to see it, even the kids. We just smell the flower and talk about how glad we are that Spring is back."

*Jim makes a point to commune with significant outdoor events:* "The first night of a snowfall, or when there's a big thunderstorm coming on, or when the moon comes up, I try to sit on the porch and just watch it. I figure if Nature's gonna put on such a good show, the least I can do is be there to see it."

*Jan watches the sunrise each morning:* "I don't do anything special, I just go out and watch it whenever I can. It makes me really glad to be alive."

*Sal does the same for the sunset:* "I try to say a little prayer each night while I watch the colors. I pray for the Earth and all the people on it."

*Jeri thinks about the birds:* "I make a point to put out seeds for them in the winter and be sure they have water in the summer. I always try to stop for a moment when I do, just to tell them thanks for being here."

*Patty makes her ritual more personal:* "I take a warm bath, filled with scented oils, just to thank my body for supporting me. It's part of Nature, too, isn't it?"

*Give your imagination free rein. Ask yourself what you'd like your ritual to communicate, which connection with the living world you'd like to honor, which of your companions you'd like to thank. Then, ask yourself how to make that statement as simply and eloquently as possible. You'll be surprised at how easy it is to come up with simple, enjoyable rituals. Start simply, focus on one thing at a time, and let your experience lead you onward.*

**c. Completion**. *Just as you opened the ritual with a gesture, mark its closing in the same way. These two gestures – even if they're as simple as a single, focused breath – reinforce your intention that everything between them be special. Your closing gesture could be a repeat of the opening one or something different – whatever feels appropriate. Choose one that helps you honor your intention and then let yourself return to normal awareness.*

**d. Action**. *Using the outline you just created, find a time to perform your ritual. Choose an appropriate setting. Take your time. Proceed with intention and as much clarity as you can. When you complete your ritual of intentional connection, take a few moments to notice how you feel. What was your experience? What have you learned? If you were to perform this practice again, is there anything you'd change? How else might you like to observe your connections with Nature?*

The benefits of intentional connection are threefold. First, by reaffirming your connection with the living world, you help antidote the alienation that comes from believing in separation. Second, by focusing your attention – and your creative energy – on your positive relationships with the living world, you make them stronger and stronger. Finally, through your practice, you feed the living world around you. Just as a child or a pet thrives when it feels your love, so does every other living being. If your practice fills you with gratitude, appreciation, respect, and beauty, you and all of life are so much richer.

Creating your own rituals to connect with Nature will bring a great deal of satisfaction. If you try it once, you'll feel good. The real value, though, comes when you practice them regularly. Whether you connect daily, weekly, or once a season, regular practice will deepen your understanding of your place in Gaia. It will fill you with purpose and inspire you with meaning. You're here not only to be this planet's brain. You're here to embody its body, heart, and soul, too.

## Experience     MEDICINE WALK

*One of the oldest ways that human beings have sought insight and self-awareness is by turning to the living world. The medicine walk is a simple technique to help you to do the same. Traditionally, a medicine walk might last a full day or longer and include fasting from food in order to increase personal clarity. You can learn the process in a much shorter time and get satisfying results. If you like it, you can always consider doing it more extensively in the future.*

***a.* Place**. *For your medicine walk, go to a natural area that feels strongly inviting. It's better to be away from human activity as much as possible, but if that isn't possible, do what you can. Before you begin, take some time to get centered and aligned both inside yourself and with your surroundings. Focus your attention by following your breath until you feel quiet and ready. Tune in to the energy of the place and ask it – verbally or silently – if it would be willing to help you. The positive feeling you get in response will be your sign to continue. If you have any doubt about the response, choose another place that feels really good.*

***b.* Intention**. *The most important part of your medicine walk is the clarity of your intention. To set your intention clearly, think of a question around which you'd like insight. It could relate to any area of your life. The more specific you make your question, the clearer the answer you'll get.*

*When you've chosen your question, turn your attention back to the living environment around you. Either aloud or silently, ask this place and the creatures within it to help you gain insight around your question. Say the question aloud, at least once, to help yourself be as clear as possible.*

***c.* Listen**. *When you feel ready, start to walk. Take all the time you like. Keeping silent will help you to maintain your focus on the question.*

*As you walk, release any expectations about what you think you should find. Follow your impulses and let them guide you to whatever calls you. When something attracts your attention, sit with it. See what it has to share with you about your question. How do you feel when you're with it? What insights come to you?*

*The medicine walk draws on your imagination and symbolic awareness. The answers you receive probably won't come verbally or literally. Instead, approach this communication as you might approach a dream or a painting. Let it speak to the intuitive, nonverbal parts of your awareness.*

*Examples:*

*Jean found herself drawn to a small stream:* "I sat beside it and felt the sounds of the water fill me with a sense of well-being. I could almost make out words –'welcome, welcome, we're here, we're here, welcome, welcome.' It was like a song just below the level of my awareness. I felt really good as I continued the walk."

*Randy talked about the trees:* "The trees all felt so self-contained. None of them seemed to have any question about whether they were doing things right or whether they had a right to be there. I realized I might try to be that way myself and just do what feels right instead of worrying about what other people say all the time."

*Joel sat on a hillside and communed:* "I picked up a stone and just looked at it for a long time. It seemed to have something to say, though at first I couldn't tell what. Then I started to look at the lines. For a minute, I could see the outline of a lion, which made me think I could try listening more closely to my own heart. Tears came to my eyes when I had that thought, so I know it was right. I was really thankful when I put the stone back in its place."

**d. Gratitude.** *When you feel complete with your medicine walk, take a few moments to thank the place for the insights you've received. If you like, use a simple, symbolic gesture to communicate your gratitude. This helps to complete your process and lets you return to the rest of your life with greater clarity. Breathe consciously and take a few moments to re-center yourself before you return to normal awareness.*

*If you've received clear answers, write them into your Nature journal. If your experience was less focused, record it anyway. In either case, allow yourself to stay open. Sometimes, the most dramatic insights come to people after they've completed their medicine walk – either in dreams or at other times.*

## Chapter 13

# NATURE CONSCIOUSNESS

Several years ago, I read an interview with a Hopi elder who spoke about the traditional methods for planting corn he'd learned in his youth. Even though their environment is extremely dry, the Hopi generally didn't water the seeds or the growing plants – yet they still produced strong, healthy corn to feed themselves. Traditional planting methods, he said, are deeply connected with the people's spiritual practices and involve talking and singing to the seeds. He lamented the fact that as fewer young members of the tribe were learning to use the traditional songs, the corn itself *was forgetting how to listen!* How different this view is from that of 'modern' farmers!

Around the same time, many miles to the southeast in Belize, a traditional Maya healer named Don Elijio Panti was sharing his herbal knowledge with Dr. Rosita Arvigo. With her help, he also shared what he'd learned with botanists, who took many of the plants to be tested for active ingredients at the National Cancer Institute. Although they found promising compounds in some of the plants, others failed to produce the expected results. When asked why the scientists couldn't find anything significant about plants he'd been using successfully for many years, Don Elijio replied that they weren't using the plants in the same way. Part of his healing process included talking to the plants as he harvested them and asking for their help with specific healings.

The words of these two elders would be quickly dismissed as 'primitive superstition' by a lot of people in our society, yet they echo the teachings of traditional herbalists and healers from around the planet. In order to work successfully with the medicine of plants, they say, it's necessary to cultivate a strong relationship with the 'spirits' associated with them. Although the words and details vary, the core beliefs about nature spirit energies are widespread and in strong agreement from place to place – so much so that we might view them as a different sort of healing technology. Could you look at the world from this perspective? Consider a related story – the tale of the Findhorn Garden.

In 1962, Peter and Eileen Caddy and Dorothy Maclean founded the Findhorn Community in northeast Scotland. All three had followed paths of strong spiritual discipline for many years and were dedicated to listening for – and actually following – intuitive guidance. In the beginning, conditions at Findhorn were quite challenging and the three founders depended on their small garden for much of their food. In an attempt to make their efforts more effective, Dorothy Maclean opened herself in meditation to the overlighting spirits or 'devas' of the garden and began to receive messages from them. One of the first said:

"Yes, you can cooperate in the garden. Begin by thinking about the nature spirits, the higher overlighting nature spirits, and tune into them. That will be so unusual as to draw their interest here. They will be overjoyed to find some members of the human race eager for their help. This is the first step.

"Just be open and seek into the glorious realms of nature with sympathy and understanding, knowing that these beings are of the Light, willing to help..."

Pursuing these meditations, she received very specific instructions regarding the garden, which quickly brought phenomenal results. Within a short time, the Findhorn Garden was known around the world for producing enormous, healthy vegetables (including some very famous 40 lb. cabbages) from sandy, barren soil under inhospitable conditions. Dorothy Maclean's initial work with the garden devas expanded to include profound, inspiring guidance from other sources in Nature. Listen to what the deva of the Scots Pine shared about the role of trees:

"We are guardians of the Earth in many ways, and humans should be a part of what we guard. We are not active young things; we are, in many ways, like a school of benevolent philosophers with unhuman purity and a great wish to serve humanity. Trees are vital to man and to life on this planet, and we are eager to experience this contact with some of you humans before the others of your kind destroy all that trees have built up."

According to Dorothy Maclean, devas are aspects of Nature consciousness responsible for bringing energy into form. They act as intermediaries between the material world and the energetic realm that underlies it. When you attune to a specific deva or 'Nature spirit' through meditation, you're not actually connecting with the mind of an individual plant or animal; instead, you're tapping into a more generalized type of consciousness that will resonate within your being in very specific ways. If you're open to it, the interaction can be informative and deeply inspiring.

Since the groundbreaking work of Dorothy Maclean and her companions at Findhorn, many people have been learning to work together with devas and Nature spirit energies. Our efforts take many forms. Some people, like Rosita Arvigo, study traditional healing techniques passed down for many generations. Others follow in the footsteps of Dr. Bach and learn to attune with Nature spirit energies to co-create the wonderful vibrational healing of flower essences and gem elixirs. Some, like Marko Pogacnik, work with Nature spirits to bring healing to the Earth itself. Others consult the devas to create gardens that promote harmony and healing or to access the insight and inspiration these beings can offer. All these explorations are active, ongoing, and continually evolving. Our goal is to learn how to move beyond the old, harmful belief in separation and to learn – each in his or her own way – how to promote a new depth of harmony and balance within ourselves and the rest of the living world.

You, too, can take part in this exploration by learning to attune directly with the conscious energies of the Natural world. The techniques aren't difficult. In fact, you've been preparing for them throughout this journey. The following guidelines will help you begin. Let's start with a meditation to help you connect with the energies of a specific place.

## *Experience*      COMMUNION WITH PLACE

***a.* Location.** *Choose a natural setting for this exploration that feels welcoming and special, somewhere outdoors where you won't be disturbed. Find a spot that feels comfortable, and then sit and take a few moments to quiet your mind by following your breath. Tune in to all your senses. Notice the feel of this place, the special character you're aware of when you sit within it. Take your time. When you feel calm and centered, proceed with the next part of the meditation.*

***b.* Opening.** *When you're ready, greet the devas or spirit energies associated with this place. Approach them with the same respect with which you'd meet another person. Set the tone with a ritual gesture, if you like, then address them directly. Speak aloud if you can. Express your gratitude for the welcome you feel here. State the reasons you've come. Ask for help in learning to connect more deeply and consciously with the energies of Nature. Communicate whatever else you have to say.*

*Your attitude is a most important part of this connection. Devas are not 'superior' beings to be worshipped or feared. They are conscious entities, different from humans but still part of the natural realm. Your willingness to approach them as equal partners helps you to open to their presence in a new way. In my experience, if you're willing to meet them half way, the devas are almost always willing and eager to communicate.*

***c.* Listen.** *With your attention on your breath, allow your awareness to expand outwards. Imagine roots extending from your body, deep into the Earth. Imagine branches from the top of your head that extend upward into the sky. Let your awareness expand in every direction, until you feel deeply connected with this place. Then, just listen with all your senses.*

*What you perceive will be highly personal. It might be quite direct, like words or a strong image in your mind. It might come through sensations in your body or through a subtle awareness of 'presence.' It might engage your imagination or bring up feelings. Stay open to whatever you sense. Don't analyze or judge any of it yet – for now you're just gathering raw material. Later, you'll have plenty of time to evaluate your experience.*

*If something comes to you easily, stay with it. Feel free to deepen the dialog by asking questions, then listening for responses. Let it lead wherever it will. Listen and observe.*

*If you're not experiencing much at first, it might help to prime the pump a little. Ask yourself the following questions – even if they don't make a lot of sense literally, your responses might help you to fine-tune your awareness.*

- *If there were a mood to this place, what might it be? Calm? Energetic? Restless? Uplifting? Something else?*

- *If this place were a type of music, what would it be like? Rhythmic? Flowing? Frenzied? Romantic? Something else?*

- *What do you feel in your own body? Where do you feel connected with this place? Does one part of you seem more involved than others? How would you describe the connection? How does it make you feel?*

- *If the place had a voice, what might that voice sound like? What kind of tone would it have? If it were speaking, what might it say to you? How would you respond?*

*Stay with this part of the process as long as you like. Let your experience take its own form.*

*John sat with the wind on a high place in Scotland:* "'Speak your own truth,' it told me. 'Speak it with every bit of your breath. That's what you've come here to learn.' I was pretty blown away by how clearly the message came."

*Sylvie felt a general sense of well-being when she sat beside a pond near her home*: "I could feel the calm of the water urging me to let go of all the ripples in my own mind. It was like, 'don't worry, everything will be fine. We're here together, that's all that matters.'"

*Bruce likes to go to a spot on the mountain where he used to live:* "There's one place, a small cave on the side, that really calls me. It feels so much more conscious than the other spots. Each time I go there I feel welcomed, like I'm at home. There's not any fireworks to the connection, but every time I sit there I feel the burdens I've been carrying just flow away."

**d. Release.** *Before you end the communion, ask the devas if there's a way you can help them? Listen and notice what you hear. Ask as well if there's anything you can do to make future communication easier. Pay attention to the response.*

*When you feel complete, thank the devas of the place for sharing with you. Either use a ritual gesture or speak your gratitude aloud. Follow your breath back to normal awareness. Before you leave the setting, record any impressions in your Nature journal. Writing down your experiences is a good way to help yourself clarify and understand them more fully.*

When you first start, communing this way may feel new or different. Because the process helps you tune in to parts of your awareness that are very subtle, your experiences may not be exactly what you expect. In any given meditation, you may receive a lot of material – or very little. You may feel you've communicated deeply – or wonder if you're making the whole thing up. Be patient. You're moving into new territory and it will take time to get accustomed to the process. Trust your experiences. Anything that comes to you, even if it seems small or insignificant, is a step in the right direction.

Many people, once they've had a little practice with this type of interaction, start to recognize a feeling of 'sweetness,' or 'strength,' or 'clear awareness' that tells them the communion is going well. These sensations are often accompanied by insights – some of which can be very direct. With deep attunement, words, images, or impressions often seem to come of their own accord. Generally, the communion feels very centering, soothing, and reassuring. At times, it can be inspiring and truly wonderful.

Keep in mind that what you're sensing is symbolic, subjective, and very subtle. Devas don't speak English, French, or even Sanskrit. They communicate with energy – which you then translate using vocabulary and concepts that make sense to you. The communion is always a two-way interaction that involves both of you equally. What you receive may be clear, insightful, and meaningful. Let it speak to you. If there are insights, put them into practice. If there are specific suggestions, try them out. However, don't overlook your part in the process. Some days, you'll be clearer than others. Some days, your mind may color your communication with its own desires and expectations. Take what you receive with a grain of salt until you've tried it out. The more you practice, the clearer your meditations will become.

## *Experience* DEVAS

*Communing with the devas associated with plants, trees, and animals is basically an extension of what you've already experienced. Here, we'll look at how you can apply what you've learned to commune with trees. You can adapt it on your own to connect with any other part of the living world.*

***a.* Center**. *Choose a natural location with a tree, or trees, in which you feel comfortable and welcome. Let yourself be attracted to one of the trees. Move toward the tree and imagine asking its permission to commune with it. When you feel that the tree is willing, sit by it. You might lean against it or touch it in some other way, because this often strengthens your initial connection. Take a few minutes to follow your breath. Tune in to your senses until you feel calm, centered, and ready to continue.*

***b.* Connect**. *Open to the presence of the deva associated with the tree. Begin with an opening gesture to communicate your respect and intention. Express your thanks for its presence and for its willingness to share with you. Tell the deva why you'd like to communicate — for example: "I'd like to learn about you and the world of Nature so we can live more harmoniously," or, "I'd like to understand who you are and how to relate with you." You don't need to be eloquent, just as clear as you can.*

*Next, open your senses. Imagine extending your awareness into the tree. Imagine feeling its roots, trunk, branches, and leaves. How does it feel to be this tree? What are your first impressions?*

*Pay attention to your body. Where does the tree's energy resonate within you? What sensations do you notice? Do you feel light, or heavy, or warm? Does touching the tree bring up any emotions?*

# CONNECTING WITH NATURE

*If the deva could take on a physical form, what might it look like? What might its voice sound like? What sort of tone would it use?*

**c. Share**. *Ask the deva what it would like to share with you today. What can it tell you about itself or about Nature? What can it tell you about yourself? Is there insight it can offer? Is there anything it would like to share through you with the world? What else would you like to ask?*

*Once you've opened the dialog, keep your mind as calm as possible – following your breath can help – and 'listen' with as many of your senses as you can. Everyone receives this sort of communion in his or her own way. You may receive words, but often the communication isn't linear at all. Some people feel sensations in their bodies. Others see images or colors. Some feel inclined to speak in rhyme, to sing without words, or to dance. Others just have a quiet sense of meaning somewhere inside themselves. For now, just gather whatever impressions come to you.*

**d. Completion**. *When you've communed as much as you like, ask the deva if there is any way you can help it. Listen for the response. Ask if there's any way to improve your communication in the future. Ask if there is a next step you should take in your Nature connection journey.*

*Then thank the spirit energy with which you've connected and release it. Follow your breath back to normal awareness and record your impressions in your Nature journal.*

Communion with Nature isn't something you do just once. If you pursue it with intention, you'll develop lifelong relationships. Like any relationships, these will deepen and mature to the extent that you nurture them with care and attention. If you let them, they'll enrich your life with insight and inspiration.

Ask Susan. "I talked yesterday with the red raspberry plants, down in the pasture. They reminded me to approach my life with balance, to receive as well as give, and to stop pushing myself so much. The deva also said the plants could use a little manure for fertilizer. I'll get it!"

Ask Jim. "The spirit of the lake reminded me that the one constant in life is change. Look to your priorities, it seemed to say. You won't be here forever – nobody is – so don't wait for tomorrow to give your heart what it loves. Do it now."

Ask Rick. "Whenever I sit with the live oaks, they remind me to keep exploring all the parts of myself. I remember that I'm more than just my work and that there are many different things that I'm here to enjoy. I always leave with a new adventure I want to explore."

Once you connect directly with Nature consciousness, you'll embark on a journey that is uniquely personal. Let the living world help you expand your horizons. Sit with the plants as they share their healing. Sit with the animals and let them speak to the deepest parts of your being. Sit beside a stream and let it to tell you about the land it drains. Ask what it learns as it drips from the leaves, soaks into the soil, and flows forth refreshed from the springs below. Talk with the moon as it floats in the sky. Ask what it sees from its far-off perspective. Talk with the mountain. Ask about its roots and the wisdom it's gained in its long, slow life. Ask about the secrets it keeps in its coves and forested glades. Open, finally, to talk with Gaia. Expand your being until you feel the full, rich breadth of the living planet. Feel it breathe and resonate within every one of your cells. Ask what it would share with you about your own special place here.

In truth, this journey of connection is your birthright, the heritage of all who are born within this great living Earth. Slow down. Breathe deep. And open to the fullness of your own being.

## Chapter 14

# CONNECT FOR LIFE

Connecting with the living world will feed you for the rest of your life. From this point forward, the tools you've explored here will help you design your personal journey of discovery and connection. From now on, you'll call the shots. The path you follow will be up to you. The direction you take will come from within your own heart. Along the way, you'll develop your own meaningful and satisfying partnership with Nature.

Being on your own doesn't mean that you'll actually be alone. In fact, it means just the opposite. If you're open to the living world, you'll meet guides and teachers all around. You'll hear their voices in the breeze or feel their presence in the stones beneath your feet. As you learn to listen, the birds will share their secrets and the flowers their inspiration. The animals will speak to you in their many, diverse ways. You'll make human friends as well, as you meet other people exploring similar journeys. With all these new companions, you'll weave an extended community within which to share discoveries and encouragement. From now on, you can be done with separation forever and take your rightful place within the dance of all life.

As you embark on your journey, let's review a few points to help make it as rich and satisfying as possible.

- First of all, trust yourself and your own inclinations. Your connection with the living world is distinct and personal. No one else can tell you what it should look like or where your path should lead. Trust your own knowing as you sit with Nature. Ask for guidance and listen when it comes. Accept the support that is inevitably yours.
- Give yourself time. Any relationship needs to be fed. One of the best ways to feed your relationship with Nature is to continue your practice of taking Nature time. Make it a combination of structured activities and non-structured communion. Choose activities that you enjoy – hikes with friends, trips to the beach, a walk around your neighborhood each evening. Sit beneath a tree, draw a picture of a flower, find time to be quiet and alone with the living world. In this way, you will continue to receive ongoing input and inspiration.
- Follow your heart. One step on your path will lead to another. Your meditations with a flower might lead you to create a garden that promotes harmony among plants, humans, and the Earth. Your time sitting beneath a favorite oak might become a source of support you can call on whenever you need strength or clarity. The simple rituals you create to mark the seasons, phases of the moon, or significant events might expand to include a small circle of friends, and the practice you started by yourself will become a means to build life-enriching community. Let the journey lead where it will.
- Record your experiences. Maintaining your Nature journal will help you stay on course. It will give you a place to record your discoveries and save insights that might otherwise fade from awareness. It will help you hone your skills of observation and become a source of reference that tells you exactly when the daffodils bloomed last year or when the geese left the pond for their annual migration. It will direct your exploration as you jot down questions or note points that awaken your curiosity. It will remind you of the wonder you felt when you watched the baby cardinals hop from their nest for the first time or your excitement when you came upon a black snake

shedding its skin. If you let it, your Nature journal will be a touchstone that reminds you of all the joy you receive from your intentional connection with the living world.

- Start where you are. Let your journey build organically. Don't be concerned with choosing the 'right' things to investigate or feel that you need to learn everything at once. Start right here, right now, and follow the path as it unfolds. In the living world, everything is connected. Wherever you start, your path will eventually touch every other part. Each point you explore will lead to others. Each step you take will carry you to the one that naturally follows. You don't need an overall plan – just a willingness to explore whatever's right here in front of you.

## Exercise — TAKE STOCK

*As you set out on your exploration, take a moment to review the journey you've taken so far. Using your Nature journal as a guide, go back through your notes. Which parts touched you most strongly? Make a list of the points that intrigued you. Note the ones that bothered you, or piqued your curiosity, or grabbed your attention in new ways. Jot down questions you'd like to investigate further. Remind yourself of the parts you enjoyed.*

*When you've completed the review, go back through your list. If you had to choose, which of the things you've written down seems the most interesting? Which would be the most fun to explore further? Which came up over and over? Circle or put a star beside the parts of the journey that touched you the most strongly. What were they?*

- I loved feeling the energy of different things with my hands.
- Talking with the trees.
- Learning the names of the flowers in my back yard was cool.
- Meditating with the spirit of the rock. That spoke to me. I want to do it again.
- The idea of Gaia really touched me. I want to read more about it.

*When you've moved through the list, you'll have a good idea of some of your major areas of interest. With time, you'll discover others. Whenever you feel the desire to deepen your exploration, this list can serve as a source of inspiration. Add to it whenever you like. Whether it gives you something to explore directly or leads you to other interesting topics and activities, trust your impulses. Whatever calls you most strongly right in this moment is the very best place to start.*

# BROADEN YOUR EXPLORATION

One way to find inspiration on your journey is to read about what other people have discovered on theirs. While reading can't take the place of direct experience, it can offer insight, encouragement, and information to deepen your understanding and motivate your explorations. Depending on your interests, there are many places to start. Joseph Cornell and Michael D. Cohen offer valuable perspectives and practical exercises based on many years of teaching environmental awareness. Joanna Macy, John Seed, Theodore Roszak and their colleagues in deep ecology and ecopsychology will help you understand your own path as part of humanity's evolving relationship with the living world. Peter Russell and James Lovelock can deepen your understanding of Gaia. Dorothy Maclean, Eileen Caddy, ROC, and others offer powerful inspiration based on their experiences at Findhorn. Marko Pogacnik will teach you about Nature spirits and Earth healing. Michelle Small Wright, Patricia Kaminsky and Richard Katz, and many others can introduce you to the healing of flower essences and cooperation between humans and devas. My own book, *Earth Spirit Warrior*, is a more in-depth journey intended to help you take your place as an active member of the planetary body. Finally, there are thousands of books and field guides on local and regional ecology to help you increase your appreciation of the living organisms that touch you most intimately.

As you proceed, you'll see this exploration as a vital, integral part of your overall spiritual journey. Just as everything in the natural world is connected, each part of you reflects and affects each other part. Connecting with Nature will complement the insights you gain through other modes of personal exploration. If you're learning to meditate, practice yoga, or work with any form of holistic healing, you'll find that all these practices deepen your connection with the living world. Likewise, learning to access wisdom and guidance from the living world will help you develop intuition in every other part of your life. There's no way to separate one part of the whole from all the others.

In the same manner, approaching the living world with respect and integrity will elicit a similar response in return. Although it might be subtle at first, you'll notice that the world begins to feel more aware or more intentional. Different people describe the feeling in their own ways.

George says: "I can feel a sense of intelligence, as if everything around me were aware. It's not always paying attention to me, but if I take the time to slow down and tune in, I can get into the flow of it."

Jim noticed the connection through synchronicities: "I wanted to see the northern lights. I kept thinking about them. Then, one night I woke up from a deep sleep, sure that I had to go to the window. The whole sky was pink and blue and green. It was beautiful. What woke me up? I don't know, but I'm very thankful that it did."

You don't have to take this journey all by yourself. Of course sometimes you'll want the quiet and the freedom to explore Nature at your own pace. As a complement, though, you'll find that sharing experiences with like-minded people is a good way to deepen your satisfaction. You're moving into new territory here – or at least a realm of experience not talked about very much in mainstream society. The support of other people with similar outlooks and goals is invaluable. Who you meet will vary according to your situation and your interests. You may be perfectly happy to proceed on your own, with no outside support. You might like to keep your discoveries 'special' by sharing them with only a few select friends. I know two men, Greg and Mike, who make a point of getting together once a month or so just to catch up. When they do, they always meet somewhere outdoors. "How can we talk about connecting with Nature when we're rushing around in traffic or sitting inside having coffee?" asks Greg.

You might also enjoy group activities that are more organized. Most cities host a number of clubs that sponsor periodic hikes, canoe trips, or other outings in Nature. Almost all environmental organizations offer these types of activities as a way to build community and help folks learn about the environment where they live. If you're interested in meeting other people who share your interests, do a little research and find these organizations in your area. If you can't find any where you live, consider sponsoring a few activities on your own. There's nothing to lose and you might make some really good new friends.

# ACTIVITIES

Whether you continue your explorations by yourself or with others, just what are you going to do? There are a million ways to explore connecting with the living world. Let's look at a few examples of what other people have enjoyed doing, to get you in the mood for figuring out your own path. You could:

- Buy a field guide. What organisms do you find the most interesting? Birds? Fish? Caterpillars? Mushrooms? Medicinal herbs? Whichever creatures attract your attention, find a guide book and start to learn about those that live in your area. What are all the different kinds called? Where do they live? What are their habits? How do they affect people? How do our actions affect them? Complement your reading by observing the organisms firsthand. Go where they are. Watch what they do, how they live, how they interact with each other. The more you watch, the more you'll learn. The more you learn, the more you'll enjoy.

- Plant trees. You might plant one a year, just to start. Find out what thrives best in your area. When is the best time to plant it? Once you put it in the ground, water and protect it until it can survive on its own. Then, plant another, or maybe two. Within a few years, you'll have made a good start towards planting your very own forest. You'll be astonished at the satisfaction it brings you.

- Approach the world with a creative eye. Expand your Nature journal to include other creative explorations of the natural world. Use your camera to record the beauty you see around you. Capture the wonder with watercolors. Dance your appreciation for the wind that blows before a storm. Make recordings of the morning birdsong. Gather the shells you love at the beach or decorate your study with stones from special places. Compose poems to express your love of the living world. Enjoy yourself.

- Hike, camp, explore the wild places that call you. The best way to appreciate the living world is to be out where it is strongest. Visit the parks around you. Witness the natural wonders that speak to your heart. Learn how to enter the world of Nature safely and without impacting it negatively. Learn to backpack, to camp, to spend time away from 'civilization' and discover simpler, more direct ways of experiencing the world. Learn how to survive with the barest essentials, to live in harmony within the fabric of life. Explore these adventures on your own or with friends. Approach them with intention and heart and they will reward you deeply.

- Start a garden. Learning to nurture the plants you enjoy is a great way to feed the living world. Start small. Plant whatever gives you the most pleasure – flowers, trees, or vegetables. Find ways to garden that actually make the land healthier than when you started. Avoid chemicals by gardening organically. Learn which plants grow well in your area. Learn what makes the soil healthy and which plants make good companions. Find out the best ways to interact with the insects and other animals that will share the garden with you.

- Teach. Share the Nature explorations you've enjoyed with others. Children, especially, take to Nature like ducklings to water. Sharing with them helps to reawaken in our adult selves the sense of wonder and curiosity that they express quite naturally. Take them on hikes. Play at being animals. Teach them to camp, to know the trees, to plant a garden. You'll love the fact that each time you share something with others, you'll be rewarded as well – with a deeper appreciation of the joy of living in this world.

Any of the activities that help you connect with Nature will provide an ongoing education. Go easy. Don't expect to know everything all at once; after 60 years, you'll still have more to learn. Give yourself permission to make mistakes and to learn from them. You can learn from books, from other people, and from your own experiences. Ask for what you need and you'll usually get it.

## *Exercise*  BRAINSTORM

*Using the suggestions listed above as a starting point, make a list for yourself of Nature-based activities that you might find interesting. Don't worry about logistics or about how you're going to find time to do them. Just give yourself free rein to play and dream. Wouldn't it be fascinating to learn how to track wild animals? Wouldn't it be cool to grow your own food? Wouldn't it be interesting to keep a hive of bees? What calls you?*

*When you've completed your list, post it somewhere you'll see it regularly. Read it through from time to time and notice which of the activities call you with the most insistence. When you're ready, pick one and start to learn more about it. How might you start? Where could you learn more? Where might you meet other people who are already enjoying that activity? Make the time and energy it takes to get started in this activity a gift to yourself. You're worth that, right? Go for it.*

# TAKE ACTION

Somewhere along the line, your explorations of the living world will bring you to the point where you want to make changes in your lifestyle. In the big picture, humanity is living in ways that are severely out-of-balance with the natural systems that support us. We – especially those of us in the more developed countries – are using far more than our share of the global resources and therefore making a grave impact on the environment. The move toward alignment will only take place when we decide, one person at time, to live in more harmonious ways. The more deeply you connect with the living world, the more strongly you'll feel the desire to do so. A day will come – or maybe already has – when that call becomes irresistible.

There are many, many actions you can take to live in alignment with Gaia. Most of them revolve around living more simply – using fewer resources, sharing what we have, living and eating in ways that are more sustainable. Living simply doesn't mean living poorly. It just means cutting out waste and paring our lives of excess consumption in order to focus on what truly sustains us. Making such a shift takes time, but it's easy to proceed one step after another. The specific actions you choose to take are up to you – pick those that are easiest and make the most sense in the context of your life. Each step you do take will make the next one that much easier. In time, you'll make a strong, positive effect on the world.

What steps can you take? There are entire books devoted to the subject. Duane Elgin's *Voluntary Simplicity* is a classic that will provide you with a strong framework for doing so. *Small is Beautiful* by E.F. Schumacher presents the same case at the level of society and economics. *Restoring the Earth* by Kenny Ausubel will inspire you to find new ways for us all to live – and make you want to check out the Bioneers, the wonderful organization he helped to found. *50 Simple Things You Can Do to Save the Earth* will get you on the right track – and you'll be able to think of a hundred other things that would be fun and easy to do without any problem. There are hands-on programs at the Findhorn Community and other centers that will give you a practical grounding in many related topics. And these are all just a start – you can easily find many more.

The more you connect with Nature, the more you'll want to live a life that supports us all. Finding ways to do so is the most natural thing you could ever do.

## *Exercise*     ACTION

*Without doing any research at all, you already know a lot of ways you might make your life more ecologically sound. Why not list a few of them right here? Don't let yourself feel guilty for not doing them already or pressure yourself into feeling that you need to do them all right away. Those feelings will only get in the way. Just take stock for now. When you're ready, you'll be glad to make whatever changes feel right.*

***a.*** *Make a list of ten simple changes you could make to bring your own life more into alignment ecologically. You don't need to know all the specific details yet, just get your general ideas onto paper. Here are a few ideas to get you started:*

- *Grow some of your own food, organically*
- *Take public transportation one day a week*
- *Start a compost pile*
- *Ride a bicycle to do errands and get exercise*
- *Put up a birdhouse or plant a butterfly garden*
- *Advocate for more parks in your community*
- *Turn off extra lights in your house*
- *Get a car with higher gas mileage*
- *Eat more vegetables, less meat*
- *Dry your clothes on a solar dryer (i.e. clothesline)*
- *Make a donation to an environmental organization*
- *Learn easy natural techniques to support your health (and lower your doctor bills)*

*There, that's a start. Now it's your turn. List at least ten things that you might do in your own life without too much effort.*

***b.*** *Choose one. Make a commitment to do one of the things on your list, starting right now. Pick one that feels manageable. When you've made that one a regular part of your life, choose another. You'll be surprised how good* *you feel – and how much more open you are to the living world when you're actually taking actions to support it!*

# INTO THE WORLD...

We live in a time of great decision. As you stand at the portal of your next adventures, you face an important choice: What kind of world would you like to live in? Would you choose a world based on separation, one that reduces the living tapestry that sustains us to nothing more than a warehouse of ever-dwindling resources? Would you choose a world where Nature is inanimate, where humans must struggle alone to survive in a harsh and hostile environment? Would you choose a world devoid of meaning and connection? Or does your heart put forth a different vision? Would you rather create a world based on respect, understanding, and cooperation? Would you rather live where humans stand aligned and allied with every sibling species, supporting together the health of a living, conscious planet?

The choice is yours and it is ours – right now and every day. We must choose the world we would create. If we choose separation, we'll continue to support a society that wages war against our own extended body. On that path, we live – and die – alone. If, on the other hand, we choose to create a world based on respect and cooperation, we'll have allies and companions all around. We'll have access to the wisdom in the rocks and the ancient trees. We'll tap the playfulness of the otter, the healing of the green ones, and the deep embrace of the entire living planet. We'll bring our lives into line and support this Earth as we live and grow together.

You are part of this living planet and the choice you make is vital to its healing. Listen to your heart. Embrace the living world and the fullness of your being. Make your choice. Choose life!

# SUGGESTIONS FOR FURTHER READING

## AWARENESS OF NATURE – ECOPSYCHOLOGY

*Coming Back to Life: Practices to Connect Our Lives, Our World* by Joanna Macy and Molly Young Brown (Stony Creek, CT: New Society Publishers, 1998). Practical, useful exercises to increase connection with self and Earth.

*Earth Spirit Warrior: A Nature-based Guide to Authentic Living* by John R. Stowe (Findhorn Press: 2002). A personalized journey of self-discovery and empowerment for people who love the Earth and want to make a difference.

*Ecopsychology: Restoring the Earth, Healing the Mind* edited by Theodore Roszak, Mary E. Gomes, and Allen D. Kanner (San Francisco: Sierra Club Books, 1995). Important collection of writings by leading ecologists and psychologists.

*How Nature Works: Regenerating Kinship with Planet Earth* by Michael J. Cohen Ed.D. (Walpole, NH: Stillpoint Publishing, 1988). Become aware of the living Earth from the inside out. This book bridges the scientific and the spiritual in a unique and powerful way.

*Listening to Nature: How to Deepen Your Awareness of Nature* by Joseph Cornell (Nevada City, CA: Dawn Publications, 1987). Simple, effective exercises for deepening your connection with the natural world.

*Reconnecting with Nature: Finding Wellness through Restoring your Bond with the Earth* by Michael J. Cohen, Ed.D. (Corvallis, OR: Ecopress, 1997). The author's "Natural systems thinking process" takes you beyond the mind to new levels of connection with all life.

*A Sand Country Almanac* by Aldo Leopold (NY: Oxford University Press, 1949). A classic. Sketches of the natural world from a man who knew it intimately.

*Sharing Nature with Children II* by Joseph Cornell (Nevada City, CA: Dawn Publications, 1989). Wonderful. Full of playful exercises and great advice on introducing the living world to children.

*Talking to Fireflies, Shrinking the Moon: Nature Activities for All Ages* by Edward Duensing (Golden, CO: Fulcrum Publishing, 1997). Fun-filled activities for all ages that help us touch the living world more deeply.

*Thinking Like a Mountain: Towards a Council of All Being* by John Seed, Joanna Macy,

Pat Fleming, and Arne Naess (Philadelphia: New Society Publishers, 1988). This wonderful guidebook helps us redefine our identities, remember our connections with all life, and realign our lives and priorities from the inside out.

*The Voice of the Earth* by Theodore Roszak (NY: Simon and Schuster, 1992). This book lies right at the core of the ecopsychology movement – it blends ecology, psychology, and a deep look at how to regain our collective sanity.

## EARTH SPIRITUALITY

*Earth Prayers from around the World: 365 Prayers, Poems, and Invocations for Honoring the Earth* by Elizabeth Roberts and Elias Amidon (HarperSanFrancisco, 1991). Beautiful prayers from many traditions for honoring the Earth. Great source of inspiration for meditation and reflection.

*Simply Living: The Spirit of the Indigenous People* edited by Shirley Ann Jones (Novato, CA: New World Library, 1999). Collected words of indigenous people from around the planet sharing wisdom based on awareness of the natural world and the universal needs of people.

*The Green Bible* by Stephen Bede Scharper and Hilary Cunningham (NY: Lantern Books, 2002). Various sources seek the word of God to inspire us to help life flourish on the Earth.

## ECOLOGICAL LIVING

*50 Simple Things You Can Do to Save the Earth* by the Earth Works Group (Berkeley, CA: Earth Works Press, 1989). The title says it all. Basic and good.

*Gaia: An Atlas of Planet Management* edited by Dr. Norman Myers (Garden City, NY: Anchor, 1993). Visual feast of facts, graphs, and pictures documenting humanity's affects on the planetary ecosystem.

*Restoring the Earth: Visionary Solutions from the Bioneers* by Kenny Ausubel (Tiburon, CA: H J Kramer, 1997). Inspiring stories of people who are actually making a difference in the world. Also check out www.bioneers.org.

*Small is Beautiful: Economics as if People Mattered* by E. F. Schumacher (NY: HarperCollins, 1989). This 1973 classic on ethical economics makes a powerful point about priorities and what is needed to make this system work for the good of all.

*Voluntary Simplicity: Toward a Way of Life that is Outwardly Simple, Inwardly Rich* by Duane Elgin (NY: Quill, revised 1993). Break out of our overly consumptive lifestyle and "live in balance to find a life with greater purpose."

*Your Money or Your Life: Transforming Your Relationship with Money and Achieving Financial Independence* by Joe Dominguez and Vicki Robin (NY: Penguin, 1993). Step by step guide to living simply and in line with your own priorities.

## ENERGETICS

*Hands of Light: A Guide to Healing Through the Human Energy Field* by Barbara Ann Brennan (NY: Bantam Books, 1987). Popular useful introduction to energy healing.

*Hands-On Spiritual Healing* (Findhorn Press, 1994 UK)/*The Healing Energy of Your Hands* (The Crossing Press, 1995 USA) by Michael Bradford . Good introduction to energetic healing, combining general principles with simple, practical techniques.

*Healing the Heart of the Earth: Restoring the Subtle Levels of Life* by Marko Pogacnik (Findhorn Press, 1998). Work with the subtle energies of the Earth itself to promote a rebalancing and restoration of planetary health.

## FINDHORN COMMUNITY

*In Search of the Magic of Findhorn* by Karin Bogliolo and Carly Newfeld (Findhorn Press, 2002). After 40 years, the Community is still strong. Here's a personal investigation of the spirit of the people who make it live.

*The Findhorn Garden: Pioneering a New Vision of Humanity and Nature in Cooperation* by The Findhorn Community (NY: HarperCollins, 1975 – or from Findhorn Press outside N. Am.). Beautifully illustrated book documents the early days of Findhorn Community and its communion with the intelligence of the nature realm.

## FLOWER ESSENCES

*The Bach Flower Remedies* by Edward Bach, MD and F.J. Wheeler, MD (New Canaan, CT: Keats Publishing, 1979). From the man who developed flower essences, a powerful treatise on healing.

*Flower Remedies Handbook* by Donna Cunningham (New York: Sterling, 1992). Good general introduction to flower essence healing.

*Flower Essence Repertory* by Patricia Kaminski and Richard Katz (Nevada City, CA: Flower Essence Society, 1987). Intro to flower essences from the perspective of those who helped start the movement in North America.

## GAIA

*Gaia: A New Look at Life on Earth* by James Lovelock (Oxford University Press, 1979). His original presentation of the Gaia hypothesis.

*The Ages of Gaia: a Biography of our Living Earth* by James Lovelock (New York: WW Norton, 1988). Presents much of the scientific evidence for the Gaia hypothesis.

*The Global Brain Awakens: Our Evolutionary Next Leap* by Peter Russell (Element Books, 2000). Fascinating discussion about emerging planetary consciousness, the importance of shifting our priorities, and implications for the future.

*The Home Planet* edited by Kevin W. Kelley for the Association of Space Explorers (New York: Addison-Wesley, 1988). Gorgeous photographs of the Earth from space, including quotes from many of the astronauts who have acted as humanity's witness to the beauty and fragility of this living planet.

## NATURAL HEALING

*Radical Healing* by Rudolph Ballantine, MD (New York: Random House, 1999). Excellent survey of holistic medical practice, with practical advice and good introductions of herbs, flower essences, Aryuveda, cleansing, and lots more.

*Sacred Plant Medicine* by Stephen Harrod Buhner (Boulder, CO: Roberts Rinehart, 1996). Herbal healing with a strong emphasis on the spirit qualities of the plants.

*Sastun: My apprenticeship with a Maya Healer* by Rosita Arvigo with Nadine Epstein (HarperSanFranciso, 1994). Fascinating story of a doctor who seeks to bridge the gap between traditional and modern medical systems.

*Staying Healthy with the Seasons* by Elson M. Haas, MD (Berkeley, CA: Celestial Arts, 1981). Good introduction to self-care and nutrition blending Western and Oriental perspectives.

## NATURE SPIRIT CONSCIOUSNESS

*Behaving as if the God in All Life Mattered: A New Age Ecology* by Michaelle Small Wright (Jeffersonton, VA: Perelandra, 1983). The author describes the path that led her to begin working with Nature consciousness and to found Perelandra Center for Nature Research.

*Communications with the Deva Kingdom* by Dorothy Maclean (Findhorn Press). Audio tape by one of Findhorn Community's founders.

*Nature Spirits and Elemental Beings* by Marko Pogacnik (Findhorn Press, 1996). Describes the author's experiences in communicating with nature spirits, elementals, and the landscape. Guidelines for healing the elemental world.

*Perelandra Garden Workbook: A Complete Guide to Gardening with Nature Intelligences* by Michaelle Small Wright (Jeffersonton, VA: Perelandra, 1987). Hands-on guide to gardening with nature consciousness.

*The Elemental Kingdom* by R. (ROC) Olgivie Crombie (Findhorn Press). Audio tape about the elemental world and our need to love and cooperate with these beings to restore the Earth.

*To Hear the Angels Sing: An Odyssey of Co-creation with the Devic Kingdom* by Dorothy Maclean (Elgin, IL: Lorian Press, 1980). The inspiring story of the birth of the Findhorn Community by one of its founders. Fascinating discussion of her explorations in communication with the nature spirits.

≈≈≈

# ACKNOWLEDGMENTS

Many people helped bring this book into being and I am deeply grateful to each one. Over the years, many teachers have shared their wisdom, understanding, and perspectives with me. Their insights infuse every part of this process. Thanks to the workshop participants (whose names have been changed) who were willing to share their personal experiences. Thanks to Matt Karol for encouragement and invaluable help with references. Thanks to Monty Schuth and Marge Stowe for unflagging support. Thanks to Karin and Thierry Bogliolo for helping to bring this book into the world. Finally, deepest gratitude to all those within the realm of Nature whose healing, support, and inspiration have guided every step of this journey.

This writing is dedicated to the living Earth.